Weekend Walks

*in the Historic
Washington, D.C. Region*

Weekend Walks

in the Historic Washington, D.C. Region

38 Self-Guided Walking Tours in the
Capital and Five Surrounding States

Robert J. Regalbuto

BACK COUNTRY

Backcountry Guides
Woodstock, Vermont

Library of Congress Cataloging-in-Publication Data:

Regalbuto, Robert J.
    Weekend walks in the historic Washington, D.C. region: 38 self-guided walking tours in the capital and five surrounding states / Robert J. Regalbuto. —1st ed.
        p.   cm.
    Includes index.
    ISBN 0-88150-597-8
    1. Washington Region—Tours. 2. Historic sites—Washington Region—Guidebooks. 3. Washington Region—History, Local. 4. Walking—Washington Region—Guidebooks. 5. Middle Atlantic States—Tours. 6. Historic sites—Middle Atlantic States—Guidebooks. 7. Middle Atlantic States—History, Local. 8. Walking—Middle Atlantic States—Guidebooks. I. Title.
    F192.3R44 2004
    917.5304'42—dc22   2003058278

Cover design by Dede Cummings Designs
Interior design by Chelsea Cloeter
Cover photo © William H. Johnson/Johnson's Photography
Maps by Moore Creative Designs, © 2004 The Countryman Press

Published by Backcountry Guides, an imprint of
The Countryman Press, P.O. Box 748,
Woodstock, Vermont 05091

Distributed by W.W. Norton & Company, Inc.,
500 Fifth Avenue, New York, NY 10110

Printed in the United States of America

10 9 8 7 6 5 4 3 2 1

To John Hinman, M.D.

Contents

III. Maryland

IV. West Virginia

V. Pennsylvania

VI. Delaware

Acknowledgments

Exploring Washington, D.C., and the surrounding region was a pleasure, both for the sights seen and for the many people I met along the way who generously shared their time and knowledge. Without their information and cooperation this guide could not have been completed, and I am very grateful.

I would be remiss not to say a word of thanks to my colleagues at the Preservation Society of Newport County for their interest and encouragement. Thanks also to Bill Murphy for his technical support on the word processor.

I am particularly grateful to Deborah Grahame for her sound advice and direction, and to Kermit Hummel, editorial director, and Jennifer Thompson, assistant production manager, both of The Countryman Press, for all that they have done to make this book possible.

My acknowledgments would be incomplete without a special word of gratitude to Dr. John Hinman. I am indebted to him for his advice and commentary on nearly every aspect of this book, and for his generosity, giving many hours of his retirement time to read and offer editorial comment on the manuscript.

Introduction

The object of walking is to relax the mind....

[W]hile you walk...divert yourself by the objects surrounding you.

Walking is the best possible exercise.

Habituate yourself to walk very far.

—*Thomas Jefferson, 1785*

This book takes Jefferson's advice a step farther. It has been written as a guide to significant sites as you walk among Washington's monuments and along the cobbled byways and country roads well beyond the district.

This guide is for a broad spectrum of readers—families and others, young and old—who have an interest in exploring the region in depth and at their own pace while benefiting from a healthy walk.

Weekend Walks in the Historic Washington, D.C. Region contains 38 distinctive, self-guided walking tours along Washington's most historic and monumental avenues as well as through picturesque neighborhoods, towns, and villages. Most walks are about 2 miles long and can be walked in a half day. Of course, each walk may be abbreviated or expanded to accommodate the walker's pace and interests. Each chapter has directions to the beginning of the walk (by car and by public transportation), an introductory overview, route directions with an accompanying map, and vignettes about places of interest you'll see. The tours include many museums and historic sites, some of which charge admission. As fees and schedules change frequently, telephone numbers and web addresses accompany the site listings so that you may access current information in planning your walk.

Whether you choose to walk in the footsteps of presidents in the Capital or venture past city limits to Civil War battlefields or picture-postcard colonial towns, along the shores of the Chesapeake Bay or in Thomas Jefferson's "academical village," this book will lead you on the best walking route and the most worthwhile destinations in each locale.

Enjoy your walking tours, and enjoy all this historic region has to offer!

I. The District of Columbia

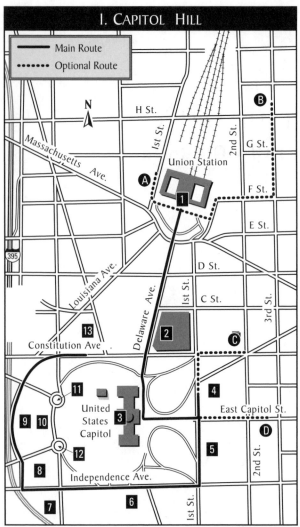

I. CAPITOL HILL

— Main Route
••••• Optional Route

N

H St.

Massachusetts Ave.

Ⓐ

Ⓑ

G St.

Union Station

F St.

1

E St.

395

Louisiana Ave.

Delaware Ave.

D St.

1st St.

C St.

3rd St.

2nd St.

2

Ⓒ

13

Constitution Ave.

4

East Capitol St.

11

Ⓓ

United States Capitol

3

9 10

12

2nd St.

8

5

1st St.

Independence Ave.

7

6

© The Countryman Press

1 · Capitol Hill

Directions: *By car:* From points west or south, take the Capital Beltway to I-66 east to US 50 east (Constitution Avenue). From points north or east, take I-95 to US 295 to US 50 west (New York Avenue). Turn left onto North Capital Street. Park at Union Station on the left. *By public transportation:* Take the Metro to the Union Station stop (202-637-7000, www.wmata.com).

Begin your tour, appropriately, at the monumental gateway to Washington, **Union Station (1).** Built in 1908 in the then-fashionable beaux-arts style according to a design by Daniel H. Burnham, the station fell into a state of decay and neglect by midcentury. Restored to its original splendor in 1988, Union Station has been retrofitted as an urban mall. Its former Turkish baths now house a nine-theater cinema, and its hall and concourses are lined with upscale shops, restaurants, and fast-food eateries. (202-371-9441, www. union-stationdc.com).

Just outside the door is the Christopher Columbus Memorial Fountain, modeled by Loredo Taft. Walk from the front door of the station straight ahead to Delaware Avenue, which leads to the Capitol.

Option A: The National Postal Museum is on the

right as you leave the station, at Massachusetts Avenue and First Street NE. A branch of the Smithsonian, the museum opened in 1993 in the old City Post Office (1914, Graham and Burnham, architects). In addition to displaying tens of thousands of rare stamps, the museum tells the story of the mail transport in the United States with exhibits featuring coaches, tracks, and airplanes. There are interactive displays, and the Discovery Center is designed specifically for children (202-357-2700, www.si.edu/postal).

Option B: The Capital Children's Museum is near Union Station at 800 Third Street NE. Opened in 1979 in a former convent and retirement home, the museum offers a wide variety of interactive educational exhibits with an emphasis on diverse cultures (202-675-4120, www.ccm.org).

As you approach the Capitol on Delaware Avenue, the **Senate Office Buildings (2)** will be on the left between C Street and Constitution Avenue. These are, from right to left, the Richard Brevard Russell Building (1909), the Everett McKinley Dirksen Building (1955), and the Philip M. Hart Building (1986). The senate office buildings are not open for touring.

Enter the **Capitol grounds (3).** Construction on the Capitol began in 1792, and the property was landscaped by Frederick Law Olmsted a century later. When Pierre L'Enfant designed the city, he planned the Capitol on this site because of its commanding position at the top of what was then known as Jenkins Hill. Originally designed by the physician-architect William Thornton, the first Capitol was much smaller than the one we see today. It contained both houses of Congress, the Library of Congress, and the Supreme Court. Burned by the British during the War of 1812, it was rebuilt, and then enlarged many times.

Enter the Capitol at the basement level. The central, round room was originally meant to be a crypt for George Washington's remains. Though Martha Washington agreed to this after her husband's demise, the plan was never realized and the first president remains buried at his home at Mount Vernon. The ceiling above the crypt at one time had a circular opening to the rotunda above.

Be sure to see the rotunda where Lincoln, Kennedy, and others have lain in state. The walls are covered with paintings by the Connecticut artist John Trumbull that depict chapters from the American Revolution. In the dome above is *The Apotheosis of Washington,* by the Italian artist Constantino Brumidi.

Visit Statuary Hall. The chamber for the House of Representatives until 1857, this room is now populated by statues of two notables from every state. On the north side of the Capitol are the Old Senate Chamber and former Supreme Court chambers. Docents provide Capitol tours, completing your visit and providing insight not only into the building but also the legislative work done within these walls (202-225-6827, www.aoc.gov).

Leave the Capitol grounds on the east side.

Option C: The Sewell-Belmont House stands at the corner of Constitution Avenue and Second Street. The oldest parts of the house date to 1680, making this the oldest dwelling on Capitol Hill. Burned in part by the British in 1814, the house survived and has been expanded and remodeled several times. This was home to the Sewell family for 123 years. In 1929 it was sold to the National Women's Party and furnished by Alva Belmont (former wife of William K. Vanderbilt and grande dame of New York and Newport society during the Gilded Age). And so it is named the Sewell-Belmont House. Filled with a large collection of memorabilia from the women's suffrage movement, the house is open to the public (202-546-3989).

From the Capitol grounds cross First Street to the **Supreme Court (4).** Built in 1935, this was one of the last great neoclassical public buildings constructed in Washington. The architect was Cass Gilbert, Jr. Ascend the steps, pass under the massive Vermont marble columns, and enter through one of the 6-ton doors. You will be in the Great Hall, which contains the busts of former chief justices. Guides direct visitors to the Court Chamber. Talks on the court, its history, and its work are given in the chamber when the court is not in session; films and exhibits are always presented on the ground floor (202-479-3211, www.supremecourtus.gov/visiting/visiting.html).

From the Supreme Court walk south one block on First Street to the Thomas Jefferson Building of the **Library of Congress (5).** It is appropriate that this building was named for our third president. When the British burned the Capitol in 1814, they did not spare its one-room, three-thousand-volume library. To replace the collection, Thomas Jefferson sold his personal library to Congress for $24,000. This, in turn, became the nucleus of the Library of Congress. Combined with the Copyright Office in 1870, the library has grown to well over one hundred million books, recordings, maps, periodicals, and other media, and the collection continues to grow, acquiring thousands of

Capitol Dome

pieces every day. Completed in 1892 (Smithmeyer, Pelz, Casey, architects), the building was inspired by the Paris Opera House. Its lavishly ornate interior required the talent and work of 26 artist-painters and 22 sculptors. The floor plan for the main reading room—a tall, octagonal room surrounded by stacks—is typical of French libraries at that time. Tours and changing exhibits are offered, and there is a shop here as well (202-707-8000, 202-707-9779, www.loc.gov).

Option D: The Folger Shakespeare Library is just around the corner and well worth a visit. From the front door of the Library of Congress (First Street) turn right. On the corner turn right onto East Capital Street. The Folger is on the right. The art deco exterior belies the 16th-century Tudor interior, where Shakespeare would feel right at home. The theater is a copy of Elizabethan models; the library (administered by Amherst College) has the world's largest collection of Shakespeare-related works. There are changing exhibits and a full calendar of plays, concerts, and readings (202-544-4600, www. folger.edu).

To resume the main tour, face the front door of the Library of Congress, turn right, and walk along First Street to the corner. Turn right onto Independence Avenue, skirting the Capitol grounds. The **House Office Buildings (6)** will be on the left. Just ahead, also on the left, is the **Bartholdi Fountain (7).** Named for its creator, Frédéric-Auguste Bartholdi (1834–1904), this fountain was modeled in 1876 for the Philadelphia Centennial Exhibition. When new it gave a water and fire presentation; it was piped for water and for gas. The gas jets have since been replaced with electric light-bulbs. Bartholdi's name probably has a familiar ring—the Frenchman later went on to model the Statue of Liberty, which was dedicated in New York Harbor in 1886.

Opposite the fountain, to your right, is the **United States Botanic Garden (8).** This, the oldest botanical garden in North America, was founded in 1820 and its first greenhouse built in 1842 on the site of the Old Patent Office Building,which is now the Smithsonian's National Portait Gallery and the National Museum of American Art. The garden was moved to this site in 1849, and in 1933 the present greenhouse was built. Renovated in 2000, it is surrounded by the 3-acre National Garden with over 12,000 plants (202-225-8333, www.nationalgarden.org).

Walk to the **Reflecting Pool (9)** between the Capitol and the Mall. In the center there is an equestrian **statue of Ulysses S. Grant (10),** the president from 1869 to 1877. Facing the Capitol, the **Peace (Naval) Monument (11)** is on the left, and a **statue of James Garfield (12),** president in 1881, on your right.

Continue clockwise on the circular path around the Capitol and cross Constitution Avenue to the **Robert A. Taft Memorial (13).** Taft was a greatly respected Senator from Ohio who was known as "Mr. Republican." His is the only monument to a U.S. Senator within the district. He died in 1953; the memorial was dedicated in 1959. The statue was modeled by Wheeler Williams. The 100-foot-high tower behind the statue houses a 27-bell carillon, which is played every fifteen minutes.

With this you have literally circled the Capitol Hill and have completed this walking tour.

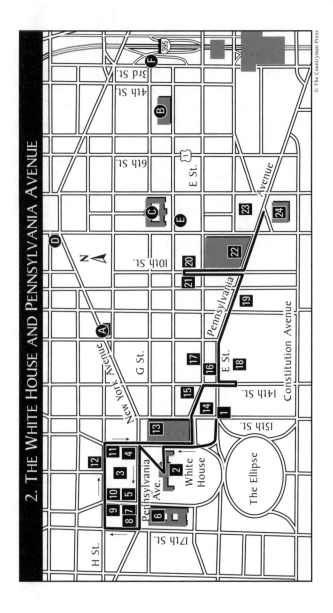

2. THE WHITE HOUSE AND PENNSYLVANIA AVENUE

2 · The White House and Pennsylvania Avenue

Directions: *By car:* From points west or south, take the Capital Beltway to I-66 east to US 50 east (Constitution Avenue). Turn left (north) onto 15th Street and follow it to the White House Visitors Center at 15th and E Streets. *By public transportation:* Take the Metro to the McPherson Square stop and walk south on 15th Street to the White House Visitors Center at E Street (202-637-7000, www.wmata.com).

For millions of Americans their first introduction to the White House was a televised tour given by Jacqueline Kennedy in 1963. In just a few short months the White House again captured the nation's attention as the first lady stood on the North Portico before following her slain husband's body to the Capitol. The scene of so many pivotal events, the White House has come to be viewed by Americans as not just the president's official residence, but as their house, too.

A White House visit should begin at the **White House Visitors Center (1)** at the southeast corner of 15th and E Streets. Admission tickets are required to tour the house; they are distributed each day on a first come, first served basis. The visitors center opens at 7:30 AM, and a maximum of four tickets are given to each person. Your tour of the White House will be self-guided. However, if you would like to participate in a guided tour, which requires a VIP ticket, contact your congressional representative's office at least four months in advance of your visit. Even if not planning a VIP tour, contact the visitors center in advance to review security requirements to avoid disappointment at the time of your visit (202-456-7041, 1-800-717-1450, www.whitehouse.gov).

The Center is an excellent place to start your visit for other reasons. There is an introductory film, as well as a presentation of Mrs. Kennedy's now legendary televised tour. There are also exhibits recounting history of the house and its first ladies.

Enter the **White House (2)** through the East Wing, off East Executive Avenue NW, just south of Pennsylvania Avenue. Pierre L'Enfant's plan for Washington included a presidential palace. James Hoban, the architect, was an Irishman who immigrated to Charleston, South Carolina. He used Dublin's Leinster Hall as his model and inspiration for the White House.

John and Abigail Adams were the first couple to live here, in 1800, and every president's family has lived in the White House since. Thomas Jefferson followed Adams and complained that the house was large enough for "two emperors, one pope, and the grand lama." In 1814 James and Dolley Madison evacuated the White House before the British torched it. Rebuilt, the building underwent major repairs in 1902, during Theodore Roosevelt's administration. In 1948 President and Mrs. Truman moved across the street to Blair House (which you will see later on this walk) while the White House was completely gutted and rebuilt. In 1961 Mrs. Kennedy issued an all points bulletin, asking that the original White House furnishings be returned for use in her restoration and redecoration plan. Over the past two centuries the house has not only been rebuilt and renovated, but also expanded; today it has 132 rooms.

About 1.5 million people visit the White House annually. The self-guided tour leads through the largest and most beautiful chambers in the house. After entering the East Wing you'll see the Vermeil Room and Library. The East Room is next, the largest room in the house. Both Lincoln and Kennedy lay in state here. Note the full-length portrait of George Washington, the only object in the house to survive the 1814 fire. Dolley Madison removed it and took it with her when fleeing the city. The tour then goes through the Green, Blue, Red, and State Dining Room, and finally the Cross Hall. Exit the house through the North Portico, which faces Pennsylvania Avenue.

Lafayette Square (3) is directly across the avenue. Originally the 7-acre park was attached to the grounds of the president's palace. Thomas Jefferson thought this was an extensively large property for the home of the president of a republic, and so now Pennsylvania Avenue separates the square from the White House grounds. In 1824 the park was named in honor of the Revolutionary War hero the Marquis de Lafayette following his triumphal visit to Washington. In the 1850s architect Andrew Jackson Downing landscaped the park. The equestrian statue in the square's center depicts President Andrew Jackson. He is flanked by statues of two French heroes of the American Revolution:

WASHINGTON, DC CONVENTION & TOURISM CORPORATION

The White House

Lafayette (4) on the right and **Count Jean-Baptiste Rochambeau (5)** on the left.

Walk west on Pennsylvania Avenue. As you approach 17th Street the **Eisenhower Executive Office Building (6)** will be on the left. When completed in 1888, this General Grant, or Second Empire, style office building was the world's largest. It was originally known as the State, War, and Navy Building, and then as the Old Executive Office Building (OEOB). In 2002 it was renamed for our 34th president. To make tour reservations call (202) 395-5895.

Opposite the Old Executive Office Building, on the right, is **Blair House (7),** 1651 Pennsylvania Avenue. The house was built in 1824 for Dr. Joseph Lovell, the first Surgeon General. In 1836 Francis Preston Blair Sr. bought the house; his heirs sold the house to the United States government in 1942. President and Mrs. Harry Truman lived here from 1948 to 1951 while the White House was being renovated. On November 1, 1950, two armed Puerto Rican nationalists broke into Blair House and attempted to assassinate the president. A guard was killed; the president was unharmed. A plaque on the fence commemorates the event. Completely renovated in 1982, Blair House is used by the president as a guest-house for visiting dignitaries. It is not open to the public.

The **Renwick Gallery (8)** is just a few steps away on the right. Built in 1859, this was originally the Corcoran Gallery of Art. Now a Smithsonian museum, the Second Empire building has been named after its architect, James Renwick, who also designed the Smithsonian Castle and New York's St. Patrick's Cathedral. The Renwick has permanent and changing exhibits on American crafts (202-257-2700, www.nmaa-ryder.si.edu/collections/index.html).

On leaving the Renwick turn right onto 17th Street and then right again at the next corner onto H Street. **Decatur House (9)** will be on the right at the corner of Jackson Place. This Federal house was built in 1819. It is the work of Benjamin Latrobe, one of America's earliest and best-known professional architects. Built for Commodore Stephen Decatur, a hero of the War of 1812, the house was lived in by a succession of statesmen, including Martin Van Buren and Henry Clay. In the 1870s it was acquired by General Edward Fitzgerald Beale, who helped open the American West. The rooms on the first floor are furnished with Federal period pieces and those on the second floor contain 19th- and 20th-century Beale family furnishings and memorabilia.Now a property of the National Trust for Historic Preservation, it is open to the public (202-842-4210, www.decaturhouse.org).

From Decatur House walk east on H Street past Lafayette Square. Facing the square, on your right you'll see two more monuments to American Revolutionary War heroes: German **Baron Frederick von Stuben (10)** on the right and Polish **General Thaddeus Kosciuszko (11)** in the far corner of the square.

Stop at the corner of H and 16th Streets. **St. John's Church (12)** will be on your left. An 1816 Latrobe design, the yellow Greek Revival Episcopal church has been altered and expanded over the years. Most notable are its stained glass windows, the oldest of which were designed by Madame Veuve Lorin, the curator for Chartres Cathedral's windows. It is known as the Church of the Presidents; every chief executive since James Madison has attended a service here. Pew number 54 is reserved for the first family (202-347-8766).

Option A: The National Museum of Women in the Arts is a short detour, three blocks east on H Street, at the corner of H Street, 13th Street, and New York Avenue. The museum is housed in the Masonic Temple completed in 1908 (Waddy B. Wood, architect) and renovated in 1987. Founded in 1981, NMWA has both exhibition galleries and a library (202-783-5000, www.nmwa.org).

The main tour continues. Stand at the corner of H and 15th Streets. Walk south along Lafayette Square. After crossing Pennsylvania Avenue walk south on East Executive Avenue. The White House will be on the right and the **Treasury Building (13)** on the left. This is the third Treasury Building to stand on this site. The first two burned in 1814 and 1833. The present fireproof building was begun in 1838 and was expanded in the 1860s. Unfortunately, the building obstructs what once was a clear view up Pennsylvania Avenue from the White House to the Capitol. A statue of Alexander

Hamilton, first Secretary of the Treasury (1789–1795), stands at the building's south end. Opposite Hamilton, in the park, stands a statue of Civil War General William Tecumseh Sherman.

With your back to the Treasury Building and facing the statue of Sherman, **Pershing Park (14)** is on the left. The park was dedicated in 1981 to General John Joseph "Black Jack" Pershing, the Commander of the American Expeditionary Forces in Europe during World War I.

The **Willard Hotel (15)** stands at the northwest corner of Pennsylvania Avenue and 14th Street. There has been a hotel on this site since 1847. The present one was designed by Henry Hardenbergh (architect for New York's Plaza Hotel) in the beaux arts style and built in 1901. The Willard was renovated between 1979 and 1986. It is often called the "hotel of presidents" because a number of chief executives have lodged here, especially on the eve of their inauguration day. Martin Luther King, Jr., completed his "I have a dream" speech in his room at the Willard before delivering it at the Lincoln Memorial. A copy of the speech is buried in a time capsule across Pennsylvania Avenue in **Freedom Plaza (16).** The plaza also has a stone map of Washington as planned by Pierre L'Enfant and a statue dedicated to Count Casimir Pulaski, a Polish general who died from wounds sustained while fighting in the American Revolution.

Opposite Freedom Plaza is the **National Theatre (17).** In 1835 the first of a series of six theaters was built on this spot. The present one dates to 1922. An urban mall, the Shops at National Place, was added in 1982 (202-628-6161, www.nationaltheatre.org).

Walk south on 14th Street. Enter the **Ronald Reagan Building and International Trade Center (18)** from 14th Street. Completed in 1998, this is the nation's second largest government building (only the Pentagon is larger). Visit the food court (Lower Level C), which in turn will lead you to the 4-acre Woodrow Wilson Plaza. On returning to 14th Street turn left. The National Aquarium will be on the right in the basement of the Department of Commerce's Herbert Clark Hoover Building. Opened in 1873, this is the oldest aquarium in the nation, and it includes a shop and a restaurant (202-482-2825).

From the National Aquarium return to Pennsylvania Avenue and walk east. Just beyond 12th Street the **Old Post Office Building (19)** will be on the right. Built in 1899, this Romanesque Revival building was restored in 1982. It now houses the the Pavilion, a complex of fast-food eateries and souvenir shops. The tower rises 315 feet and is second in height only to the Washington Monument. The tower's observation deck is a well-kept secret. Forgoing the lines and long waits at the Washington Monument, visitors may enjoy nearly-as-good panoramic views from the tower, which, thankfully, is elevator accessible (202-289-4224, www.old-postofficedc.com).

With your back to the Post Office turn right and walk along Pennsylvania Avenue to the next corner (10th Street). Turn left, crossing Pennsylvania Avenue and walking a block and a half up 10th to **Ford's Theatre (20)** on the right at 511 10th Street NW. The theater was built in 1863 and just two years later gained an infamous place in history as the spot where Abraham Lincoln was shot by John Wilkes Booth on April 14, 1865.

Restored in 1968, the theater is maintained by the National Park Service. Start your visit in the basement where Lincoln (and Booth) memorabilia are on exhibit. Then go upstairs to the auditorium. Park rangers present talks every half hour. Ford's Theatre today is not just a museum but also a functioning theater, where plays are staged (202-426-6924, www.nps.gov/foth).

After he was shot Lincoln was carried to the Petersen house across the street. He died there the following morning. Also known as the **House Where Lincoln Died (21),** it is open to the public. Tour information is available at Ford's Theatre.

Retrace your steps down 10th Street to Pennsylvania Avenue. The large, imposing, concrete building on the left is the **J. Edgar Hoover F.B.I. Building (22),** constructed in 1974 and designed by C. F. Murphy. Tours are given and visitors are shown memorabilia of notorious criminals as well as weapons and the serology and fingerprints labs. The tour culminates with a marksmanship demonstration (202-324-3437).

On leaving the F.B.I. Building turn left onto Pennsylvania Avenue and walk one block. Market Square, a complex of offices and restaurants built in 1990 (Hartman-Cox and Morris, architects), is on the left. The nucleus of Market Square is the **U.S. Naval Memorial and Naval Heritage Center (23),** which was designed by Conklin Rossant. The granite map on the exterior is the world's largest. The statue *Lone Sailor* was modeled by Stanley Bleifeld. The interior contains the Naval Memorial Log Room, a gallery of interactive exhibits, and film presentations in the Burke Theater (202-628-3557, www.lonesailor.org).

The **National Archives (24)** is just across Pennsylvania Avenue. Completed in 1935, this is a John Russell Pope design. Step inside and view the nation's founding documents and other papers that are carefully enshrined, including the Declaration of Independence (1776), the Constitution (1789), and the Bill of Rights (1791) (202-501-5400, www.nara.gov).

The tour ends here. The nearest Metro stop is the Archives–Navy Memorial station.

Option B: The **National Building Museum** is four and a half blocks from the Archives. Walk north on Seventh Street and then east on F Street. The museum will be on the left between Fourth and Fifth Streets. Built as the Pension Building between 1881–87, the exterior is wrapped in a 1,200-foot-long terra cotta frieze depicting an unending parade of soldiers and sailors. But the best is inside. The Great Hall, the length of a football field, rises 15 stories. While the building itself is worth a visit, there are also exhibits on architectural history which are worth viewing (202-272-2448, www.nbm.org).

At the virtual doorstep of the National Building Museum you'll see the **National Law Enforcement Officers Memorial,** dedicated by President George H. W. Bush in 1991. A museum is planned, to be built one block to the south. Until then, there is a visitors center at 605 E Street NW (202-737-3400, www.nleomf.com).

The Judiciary Square Metro stop is at the National Building Museum and the Law Enforcement Officers Memorial.

Option C: Two Smithsonian Museums in the neighborhood—the **National Portrait Gallery** and the **National Museum of American Art**—are both located in the Old Patent Office Building (1836) on the block bordered by F and G Streets and Seventh and

Ninth Streets, at the Gallery Place–Chinatown Metro stop. As this book goes to press the museums are undergoing a $400 million renovation (202-357-2000, 202-357-2020, www.si.edu).

Option D: The **City Museum,** opened by the Historical Society of Washington, D.C., is located at 801 K Street (between Seventh and Ninth Streets, across from the Convention Center) (202-383-1800, www.hswdc.org).

Option E: A newer museum is nearby: the **International Spy Museum** at 800 F Street (between Eighth and Ninth Streets). The museum also includes a restaurant (202-EYE-SPY-U, www.spymuseum.org).

Option F: The Lillian and Albert Small Jewish Museum is at 701 Third Street NW, near G Street. Housed in the district's oldest synagogue, the **Adas Israel Synagogue,** built in 1876, the museum relates the history of Jews in the Washington area and their contributions (202-789-0900).

3. THE MUSEUMS ON THE MALL

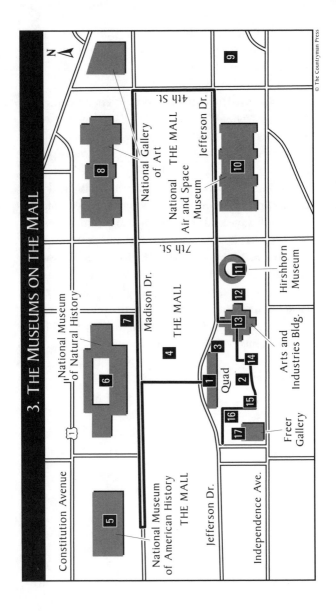

Constitution Avenue

I-1

National Museum
of Natural History

National Museum
of American History
THE MALL

Jefferson Dr.

Madison Dr.

THE MALL

Quad

Arts and
Industries Bldg.

Freer
Gallery

Independence Ave.

National Gallery
of Art

4th St.

7th St.

THE MALL

National
Air and Space
Museum

Jefferson Dr.

Hirshhorn Museum

N

© The Countryman Press

3 · The Museums on the Mall

Directions: *By car:* From points west or south, take the Capital Beltway to I-66 east to US 50 east (Constitution Avenue). Turn right (south) onto 14th Street to the Smithsonian Castle. From points north or east, take I-95 to US 295 to US 50 west (New York Avenue). Turn left (south) onto 14th Street to the Smithsonian Castle. *By public transportation:* Take the Metro to the Smithsonian stop and exit at the Mall (202-637-7000, www.wmata.com).

This walking tour encompasses museums, galleries, and gardens belonging to the Smithsonian Institution, as well as the National Gallery of Art. The story of the Smithsonian is in itself fascinating. The institute is named for an English scientist, James Smithson (1765–1829). When Smithson died in Italy his fortune went to a nephew. His nephew died in 1835 and the inheritance went, according to Smithson's wishes, to the United States of America, to found in Washington, under the name of the Smithsonian Institution, "an establishment for the increase and diffusion of knowledge." Established by Congress in 1846, the Smithsonian Institute at first focused on scientific research, and then later developed its museums. Smithson's initial

WASHINGTON, DC CONVENTION & TOURISM CORPORATION

Smithsonian Castle

bequest of a half million dollars has been supplement-
ed by other gifts, and the Smithsonian has grown into
the largest museum group in the world, encompassing
16 museums, 2 study centers, 4 gardens, and a zoo.
About 140 million objects are in the Smithsonian's collection. Most of the museums are open daily from

10:00 AM to 5:30 PM (202-357-2700, 202-357-2020, www.si.edu). Admission is free.

This tour begins at the Smithsonian's oldest building, the **Castle (1).** Designed by James Renwick (who also designed New York's St. Patrick's Cathedral), the Castle was completed in 1855. The exterior is red sandstone from Maryland, and the architectural style may be labeled as 12th-century Norman, while incorporating Romanesque and early Gothic details. When built the Castle contained the entire institute: its offices, library, exhibition space, and even the living quarters for its staff. Step inside. The body of James Smithson lies in the crypt. It was exhumed from the English Cemetery in Genoa, Italy, in 1904. Interestingly, Smithson never visited America in life. The Castle is also the Smithsonian's Information Center, and so this is an ideal place to begin your tour.

Before moving on, you may want to visit two gardens just outside the Castle door. On the south side is the **Enid A. Haupt Garden (2),** a 4-acre re-creation of a Victorian garden. On the opposite side of the Castle, on the Mall and just to the east, is the **Katherine Dulin Folger Rose Garden (3).**

Exit the Castle on the Mall (north) side, cross the **National Mall (4)** on the footpath, and turn left. The **National Museum of American History (5),** the Behring Center, completed in 1964 (Steinman, Cain, and White, architects), is the first stop on the Mall's north side. Don't be put off by the museum's forbidding exterior. Inside is the most fascinating collection of Americana gathered anywhere. Some highlights among the museum's 16-million-object collection are the Star-Spangled Banner that flew over Baltimore's Fort

McHenry as Francis Scott Key penned the national anthem; a collection of gowns worn by first ladies at inaugural balls and other fetes; the Model T Ford; and exhibits on transportation, agriculture, and other aspects of American history, life, and culture.

After exploring the National Museum of American History exit on the Mall side, turn left, and walk one block to the **National Museum of Natural History (6).** This was the Smithsonian's third building, completed after the Castle (1855) and the Arts and Industries Building (1881). Built in 1911 (Hornblower and Marshall, architects), this neoclassical structure was expanded in 1965 and houses many treasures, including the Hope diamond, dinosaur skeletons, dozens of interactive exhibits, the O. Orkin Insect Zoo, an IMAX Theatre, a cafe, and a gift shop. In 2003 the $31-million Hall of Mammals was completed and unveiled.

Return to the Mall and turn left; the **Butterfly Habitat Garden (7)** will be on the left. Interpretive signs identify the plants and insects. You will pass the ice skating rink on the way to the **National Gallery of Art (8).** The nucleus of the museum's collection was acquired by financier Andrew W. Mellon in 1931. He purchased a magnificent collection that had been in imperial Russia from the Soviets for $6 million. His collection grew to include 126 paintings, which he presented to the United States as well as a building in which to house them. The West Building was designed by John Russell Pope and completed in 1941. Its rotunda is probably one of the most beautifully serene interiors in the city. The East Building, designed by I. M. Pei, was added in 1978 and houses contemporary art. Mellon's initial bequest has grown to include over 100,000

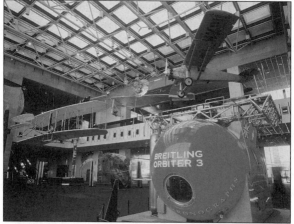

National Air & Space Museum

CAROLYN RUSSO, © SMITHSONIAN INSTITUTION

works. The holdings encompass the most extensive collection of Italian art in America (including *Ginevra de Benci*, the only oil painting by Leonardo da Vinci in the Western Hemisphere), Flemish, German, Dutch, French, and British paintings, sculpture, prints, drawings, and decorative arts. American artists are well represented with works by Gilbert Stuart, Rembrandt Peale, Winslow Homer, James McNeill Whistler, John Singer Sargent, and others. The Gallery has restaurants and a large shop (202-737-4215, 202-842-6176, www.nga.gov).

Leave the National Gallery on the Mall side and walk south on Fourth Street, crossing the Mall. The Capitol is on the left. Just ahead on the left is the site of the Smithsonian's **National Museum of the American Indian (9).** At the time of this writing the museum is under construction with a completion date of 2004. In 1989 an act of Congress established this, the first national museum dedicated to the "preservation, study, and exhibition of the life, languages, literature, history, and arts of Native Americans." The $219 million facility will house a collection of 800,000 objects, and its landscaping will include native plants, a wetlands area, and a waterfall. An on-site visitors center is now open with models of the soon-to-be museum and a window to the construction site.

Facing the Mall turn left and walk to the **National Air and Space Museum (10),** which opened its doors during the 1976 bicentennial year. Note that the Tennessee marble on its exterior matches the marble on the facade of the National Gallery of Art across the Mall. This is said to be the most visited museum in the world, attracting over 10 million visitors annually. Its 23 galleries display 240 aircraft, 50 missiles and rockets, and dozens of hands-on interactive exhibits. There is also the Samuel P. Langley IMAX Theatre, shops, and a restaurant. Two outstanding pieces in the collection are Lindbergh's *Spirit of St. Louis* and the Wright brothers' century-old *Flyer*.

Continue walking along the Mall. The large, circular building on your left is the **Hirshhorn Museum (11).** Joseph Hirshhorn (1899–1981) donated 6,000 pieces of 20th-century sculpture to the Smithsonian, and this donut-shaped building and its garden were constructed here in 1974 to display them. The museum includes a broad spectrum of works, from Rodin to contemporary artists.

Tucked between the Hirshhorn Museum and the Arts and Industries Building is the **Mary Livingston Ripley Garden (12),** which is planted with bulbs and other seasonal flora.

The **Arts and Industries Building (13)** was completed in 1881 to give a more permanent home to the machinery and other objects exhibited at the 1876 Centennial Exposition in Philadelphia. In the 1960s the collection was moved to the American History Museum across the Mall. The Arts and Industries Building was restored in time for the Bicentennial in 1976. Today it is used for special exhibits and to house a children's Discovery Theater.

Just west of the Arts and Industries Building is the Castle on the right and the entrance to the underground **African Art Museum (14)** on the left. The Haupt Garden is between them. The museum was founded in 1964, joined the Smithsonian in 1979, and moved into its present underground facility in 1987. It is interesting to note that the previous home for the collection was the Washington, D.C., home of the former slave and famous abolitionist Frederick Douglass. The museum has a collection of more than 6,000 objects.

Next is the **Arthur M. Sackler Gallery (15).** Its aboveground entryway mirrors the African Art Museum's; its galleries are also subterranean. Both museums are linked underground. The Sackler collection features 1,000 works of art from Asia and the Near East, including paintings, bronzes, jade, and lacquerware. Dr. Arthur M. Sackler, a publisher of medical literature and a psychiatrist, collected the works and presented them to the Smithsonian. Both museums are also connected to the underground **S. Dillon Ripley Center (16)** where special exhibits are mounted.

Continuing west on the Mall, the **Freer Gallery of Art (17)** is next. Founded by Charles Lang Freer, the gallery houses James McNeill Whistler's *Peacock Room* and works by Winslow Homer, John Singer Sargent, and other American artists. The Freer also includes one of the world's finest collections of Asian art. All are housed in a 1923 reproduction of a Florentine Renaissance palazzo.

With that you have walked full circle, visiting the museums on the Mall.

4 • Major Monuments and More

Directions: *By car:* From points west or south, take the Capital Beltway to I-66 east to US 50 east (Constitution Avenue). The Ellipse will be on the left between 17th and 15th Streets. From points north or east, take I-95 to US 295 to US 50 west (New York Avenue). Turn left (south) onto 15th Street. The Ellipse will be on the right. *By public transportation:* Take the Metro to the Federal Triangle stop and walk west two blocks on Constitution or Pennsylvania Avenue (202-637-7000, www. wmata.com).

This walking tour will concentrate on the larger monuments on the Mall and will also allow you the opportunity to visit museums and other significant points of interest along the way. Start at the **Ellipse (1)**—a 54-acre park that lies between the White House grounds and the Mall. Pierre L'Enfant envisioned this as a part of the White House (or presidential palace) grounds. The marshy acreage became an army camp and a corral for horses during the Civil War. In 1880 landscape architect Andrew Jackson Downing designed the park as we see it today. At the north end of the

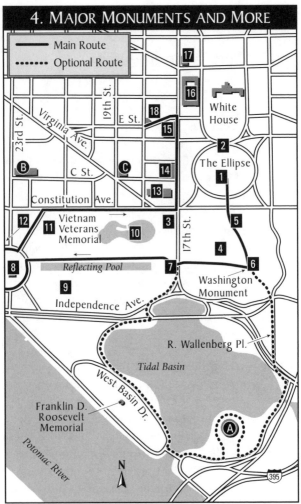

4. MAJOR MONUMENTS AND MORE

— Main Route
····· Optional Route

17

16

White House

2

The Ellipse

1

23rd St.

19th St.

Virginia Ave.

E St.

18

15

B

C St.

C

14

Constitution Ave.

13

5

4

6

12

Vietnam Veterans Memorial

11

3

10

17th St.

8

Reflecting Pool

7

Washington Monument

9

Independence Ave.

R. Wallenberg Pl.

Tidal Basin

West Basin Dr.

Franklin D. Roosevelt Memorial

A

Potomac River

N

395

© The Countryman Press

Ellipse, just across the street from the White House, is the **Zero Milestone (2).** Placed here in 1920, the 4-foot-high pink granite column is the official starting point for distances measured from Washington. Every year the National Christmas Tree is placed just a few feet to the south.

Walk south to Constitution Avenue, the former site of the Tiber Canal. The **fieldstone cottage (3)** at the southwest corner of Constitution Avenue and 17th Street is the former lockkeeper's house, built about 1835. The lockkeeper collected tolls on the canal. The building is now a toolshed.

Cross Constitution Avenue and walk across the **National Mall (4)** on 15th Street. To the right is the **German Friendship Garden (5).** Dedicated in 1983, the garden commemorates the arrival of the first German immigrants in America in 1683. The garden includes seasonal plantings, two fountains, and six garden benches, and was funded by American and Canadian citizens.

The Mall was another of L'Enfant's pivotal plans for the capital city, providing a grand, spacious, 2-mile vista from the Capitol on Jenkin's Hill in the east to the Potomac River in the west. Throughout the 19th century the Mall remained a marshy, undeveloped space dotted with the occasional lumberyard. The old rail terminal sat right in the center. In 1902 Michigan senator James McMillan initiated the development of the Mall to what we enjoy today. Union Station replaced the old rail terminal, the Lincoln Memorial was built in the 1920s, and extensive landscaping was done.

Approach the **Washington Monument (6).** From the very start, L'Enfant planned a central monument to

Jefferson Memorial

George Washington. His vision of an equestrian statue was transformed into an elaborate temple, conceived by architect Robert Mills in 1847. While Mills remained the architect, his plans were modified to the stark obelisk we see today. The monument was to stand on the Ellipse, but the soil there was too unstable. The cornerstone was laid in 1848. Construction was slow and then was halted completely during the Civil War when the obelisk was just one quarter its proposed height. Building resumed in 1880. (Note the two shades of marble used before and after 1880.) Completed in 1885, the Washington Monument stands 555 feet high. By law, no building in Washington may be taller. Step inside and take the elevator to the top to enjoy the panoramic views of the city and surrounding countryside (202-426-6841, www.nps.gov/wamo).

Option A: Looking south, the circular temple in the

distance is the Jefferson Memorial (202-426-6841, www.nps.gov/thje). Designed by John Russell Pope, the memorial was dedicated in 1943. Jefferson, himself an architect, used the Pantheon in Rome as an inspiration for his rotunda at the University of Virginia and for his home, Monticello. It was appropriate then that his monument also echoes the Pantheon. It enshrines a statue of our third president wearing a fur-trimmed, full-length coat given to him by his friend General Thaddeus Kosciusko, a Polish hero of the American Revolution. You may walk around the Tidal Basin to visit the Jefferson Memorial, enjoying the sight of hundreds of Japanese cherry trees along the way, some of which are pictured on this book's cover. To do this, walk east from the Washington Monument and join the path heading south. You will pass the Sylvan Theater on the right, an outdoor stage; the Marine Corps presents concerts here (202-619-7222). Continue south on Raoul Wallenberg Place. The U.S. Holocaust Memorial Museum will be on the left (202-488-0400, www.ushmm. org) and beyond that, also on the left, the Bureau of Engraving and Printing. Since 1862 the bureau has been responsible for printing paper currency. Today it also prints a vast array of things, from postage stamps to White House invitations. Tours are given during which visitors may see the currency printed (202-874-3019, 202-874-3188, www.moneyfactory.com). After visiting the Jefferson Memorial, continue your walk in a clockwise direction, cross the footbridge, and the Franklin Delano Roosevelt Memorial (202-619-7222, www.nps. gov/fdrm) will be ahead. From the Roosevelt Memorial, Basin Road will lead back to the Mall.

The most recent addition to the Mall is the **National**

World War II Memorial (7), situated between the Washington Monument and the east end of the reflecting pool. Authorized in 1993, construction began in 2001 with a completion date of Memorial Day, 2004. The $200-million project was funded mainly by private contributions. The design, by Friedrich St. Florian of Providence, Rhode Island, includes a plaza, reflecting pool and fountain, two pavilions, and a series of memorial columns (www.wwiimemorial.com).

Look down the length of the reflecting pool to the **Lincoln Memorial (8).** On the left is the **Korean War Veterans Memorial (9),** dedicated in 1995. The **Constitution Gardens (10)** to the right of the pool were dedicated during the bicentennial year 1976. A quiet, tree-shaded respite from the city's activity, the garden includes a footbridge that spans a pond and leads to an island with a monument dedicated to the signers of the Declaration of Independence.

Beyond the Constitution Gardens is the **Vietnam Veterans Memorial (11).** Authorized by Congress in 1980, the monument was dedicated two years later. The designer was Maya Lin who at the time was a 21-year-old architectural student at Yale University. The long, polished black marble wall is inscribed with the names of more than 58,000 men and women who died while serving in Vietnam. An index book helps visitors find the names inscribed on the wall (202-634-1568, www.nps.gov/vive).

You have reached the **Lincoln Memorial (8).** Almost immediately after Abraham Lincoln's assassination in 1865 proposals for his memorial emerged. Both the site and the design were debated. One proposal was a 72-mile highway from Washington to

rial

Gettysburg punctuated with monuments. Finally in 1913 Henry Bacon's design was approved and the site chosen. The monument resembles the Parthenon in Athens, its entrance on the broad side. The memorial's exterior is faced with Colorado Yule marble; the columns and interior are Indiana limestone. The seated Lincoln was modeled by Daniel Chester French and sculpted by the Piccirilli brothers in Genoa marble. The 19-foot-tall statue was transported here in 28 pieces. Remarkably, the statue cost a mere $46,000. The memorial was dedicated in 1922 by Supreme Court Justice (and former President) William Howard Taft. Lincoln's son, Robert Todd Lincoln, was in attendance (202-426-6895, www.nps.gov/linc).

The Lincoln Memorial has been the scene of many historic gatherings. On Easter Sunday in 1939 Marian Anderson sang to an audience of 75,000. An African American, she was denied permission to sing in the DAR's Constitution Hall. In 1963 Dr. Martin Luther

King, Jr., addressed 250,000 people with his "I have a dream" speech.

Walk around the memorial and take a look at the view across **Arlington Memorial Bridge (12)** toward Arlington National Cemetery. The bridge, modeled on the Ponte Sante Angelo, which spans the Tiber River in Rome, is guarded at either end by *The Art of Peace* and *The Art of War.* Cast and gilded in Italy, these monumental statues were a gift from the people of Italy.

Option B: The Diplomatic Reception Rooms in the State Department Building (2201 C Street at 23rd Street) are open to visitors by appointment. To reach the building from the Lincoln Memorial, walk north on 23rd Street to C Street. The rooms are decorated with nearly $100 million of the finest 18th- and 19th-century American furniture and artwork. The reception rooms are used by the president, vice president, secretary of state, and cabinet members to receive and entertain nearly 100,000 diplomats and dignitaries annually. *Note:* Tours are by appointment only and it is highly recommended that you make your reservation at least two months in advance of your visit (202-647-4000, www.state.gov).

Option C: From the Lincoln Memorial walk north on 23rd Street and then east on C Street to 19th Street to the Department of the Interior Building (1849 C Street), which has a museum worth visiting. The department was created by Congress in 1849 to help manage the nation's westward expansion. Completed in 1935 (Waddy B. Wood, architect), this Moderne building is embellished with more WPA art than any other building in the district. The museum focuses on the work of the department. Its galleries are dedicated to the

National Park Service, the Bureau of Indian Affairs, the U.S. Geological Survey, and the Bureaus of Land Management, Mines, and Reclamation. Guided tours of the rest of the building highlight its remarkable collection of 1930s WPA murals. One depicts Marian Anderson's Easter Sunday concert at the Lincoln Memorial in 1939 (202-208-3100, www.doi.gov).

From the Lincoln Memorial walk down Henry Bacon Drive and bear right onto Constitution Avenue. Between 19th and 17th Streets the **Organization of American States (13)** will be on your left. The oldest organization of nations, the OAS was founded in 1910, and its members includes 33 countries in the Western Hemisphere. The Spanish Renaissance building, dedicated in 1910, was the gift of American financier Andrew Carnegie. Visit the Art Museum of the Americas at 201 18th Street (202-458-6016), which is located in the former residence of the OAS Secretary General. A statue of the South American hero Simón Bolívar is in the park across the street.

Walk to 17th Street and turn left. The **Headquarters for the Daughters of the American Revolution (14)** will be on the left. The complex of buildings covers an entire city block. The beaux-arts-style Memorial Continental Hall faces the Ellipse. Edward Pearce Casey, one of the architects who worked on the Library of Congress, designed the building. The thirteen columns of the portico facing C Street represent the original colonies. The hall houses a museum with 33 period rooms and a genealogical research library, which Alex Haley used to help research his book *Roots*. Visitors may also see changing exhibits of American silver, glass, textiles, and ceramics. Next door is Constitution Hall. An

Washington Monument

auditorium designed by John Russell Pope, it was completed in 1939 (202-879-3254, www.dar.org).

Return to 17th Street, turn left, and walk one block to the Corcoran Gallery of Art. En route the American Red Cross Headquarters will be on the left.

The **Corcoran Gallery of Art (15)** is the largest and oldest private art museum in the district. It was founded in 1869 by banker William Wilson Corcoran and at one time was housed in what is now the Smithsonian's Renwick Gallery, at Pennsylvania Avenue and 17th Street. Completed in 1897, the present gallery was designed by Ernest Flagg and is a splendid example of beaux-arts architecture. The gallery's holdings include an exceptional collection of works by American artists, including Gilbert Stuart, John Singer Sargent, and Mary Cassatt, as well as European works. The gallery's best-known piece is a marble statue entitled *The Greek Slave,* sculpted by Hiram Powers. The painting *The Old House of Representatives* by Samuel F. B. Morse (of Morse code fame) is a highlight of the collection (202-639-1700, www.corcoran.org/cga).

On leaving the Corcoran turn left on 17th Street and walk to the corner of New York Avenue. Ahead on the right is the **Eisenhower Executive Office Building (16).** The State, War, and Navy Building (as it was first named) was built by order of President Ulysses S. Grant. Its style is Second Empire, often called "General Grant style," because of its popularity in public building during Grant's administration (1869–77). Construction began in 1871, and when completed in 1888 it was the world's largest office building. Some interesting data: There are 900 columns on the exterior, the granite walls are four and a half feet deep, and there are over 550 rooms lining two miles of corridors. The architect was Alfred B. Mullet, who also designed the **Renwick Gallery (17)** (originally the Corcoran Gallery), which stands just opposite the north end of the OEOB. Restored, the OEOB is open for tours on Saturday mornings by reservation only (202-395-5895).

Turn left onto New York Avenue and walk west for one block to the corner of 18th Street. The **Octagon (18)** on the corner is the Museum of the American Architectural Foundation. Built in 1798, its architect was William Thornton, the Capitol's first architect. This Federal-style building was one of the city's largest and most elegant residences. It survived the British burning of Washington during the War of 1812 and today is one of the oldest houses in the District. James and Dolley Madison, on returning to Washington in 1814 and finding the White House a charred ruins, took up residence in the Octagon. President Monroe signed the Treaty of Paris here, marking the end of that war. It is now restored and furnished with period pieces; visitors may see the house, its elegantly furnished rooms, and its basement-level kitchen and exhibits (202-638-3221, www.archfoundation.org/octagon).

If you retrace your steps just one block east on New York Avenue you will be at the Ellipse where this walking tour began.

5 · Georgetown

Directions: *By car:* From points west or south, take the Capital Beltway to I-66 east to US 50 east (Constitution Avenue). Turn left onto 23rd Street, go around Washington Circle, and northwest on Pennsylvania Avenue. Turn right onto 28th Street and right again onto Q Street. From points north or east, take I-95 to US 295 to US 50 west (New York Avenue). At Mt. Vernon Square turn right (northwest) onto Massachusetts Avenue to Dupont Circle. Go around the circle to P Street (west) and then turn right onto 28th Street and right again onto Q Street. Dumbarton House will be on the left at 2715 Q Street. *By public transportation:* Take the Metro to the Dupont Circle station and exit at Q Street North. Walk west on Q Street (202-637-7000, www.wmata.com).

The neighborhood we know today as Georgetown was settled in the late 1600s and became known as the Rock of Dumbarton, a part of Maryland. In the mid-1700s the town's streets were laid and its name was changed to Georgetown in honor of King George II. It was a tobacco growing community and a busy Potomac River port. In the late 18th century Georgetown was

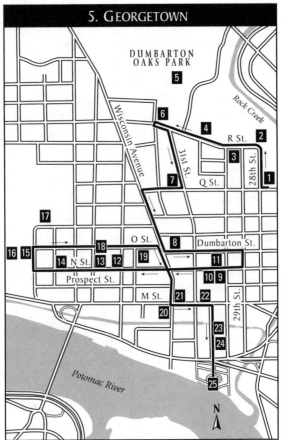

5. GEORGETOWN

DUMBARTON OAKS PARK

Rock Creek

Wisconsin Avenue

5

6

4

R St.

2

31st St.

3

28th St.

7

Q St.

1

17

O St.

8

Dumbarton St.

16 15

18

14 N St. 13 12

19

11

Prospect St.

10 9

M St.

21

22

29th St.

20

23

24

Potomac River

25

N

© The Countryman Press

carved from Maryland and became part of the District of Columbia. Georgetown's growth and development was checked by a severe flood in 1890. The once fashionable neighborhood became one of the district's most notorious slums. This trend began to reverse in the 1930s. Its distinctive charm rediscovered, Georgetown began a resurgence which has continued to this day. The neighborhood's reputation was further enhanced with the presence of residents like John and Jackie Kennedy; you will see some of their homes on this walk.

The tour begins at a grand 18th century manor, **Dumbarton House (1),** at 2715 Q Street NW near 28th Street. Built in 1799, the house has been occupied by several families. In 1928 it was acquired by the National Society of the Colonial Dames of America. Under the guidance of Fiske Kimball, Dumbarton House was restored to its original Federal appearance. The NSCDA opens the house to visitors for tours (202-337-2288, www.dumbartonhouse.org).

Turn right onto 28th Street and then left onto R Street. **Oak Hill Cemetery (2)** will be on the right, its entrance at R and 30th Streets. William Wilson Corcoran (founder of the Corcoran Gallery of Art) established this cemetery in 1849. He is buried here in a replica of a Doric temple. A map of the cemetery is available at the gatehouse. Oak Hill's enchanting Gothic Revival chapel was designed in 1859 by James Renwick, the Smithsonian Castle's architect.

On the opposite side of R Street at number 2920 you'll see the **home of Katharine Graham (3),** the late publisher of the *Washington Post*. Born in 1917, she died in 2001.

Montrose Park (4) is contiguous with the cemetery, and beyond that is **Dumbarton Oaks Park (5).** Your next stop will be **Dumbarton Oaks Museum and Gardens (6)** at R and 31st Streets. A Federal mansion built in 1801 for Maryland's Senator William Dorsey, the house was expanded and embellished in the Victorian style later in the century. In 1920 Robert and Mildred Bliss bought the estate and engaged the firm of McKim, Mead, and White to restore the house and to add a music room. World travelers and collectors, the Blisses later added a museum wing to house their collections, which feature Byzantine and pre-Columbian art. In 1940 the Blisses bequeathed the house, its collections, its 14,000-volume library, and its extensive formal gardens to Harvard University. The magnificent gardens and the museum are open to the public (202-339-6410, www.doaks.org). An interesting aside: In 1944 the Dumbarton Oaks Conferences, which led to the founding of the United Nations, were held in the music room. The adjacent 27-acre Dumbarton Oaks Park was a gift from the Blisses to the United States.

After visiting Dumbarton Oaks walk south on 31st Street. **Tudor Place (7)** will be on the right at number 1644. Another Federal period house, Tudor Place was built in 1805. Its designer was the physician-architect William Thornton, who was the Capitol's first architect. The house was built for Thomas Peter, Georgetown's first mayor and the husband of Martha Custis, a great-granddaughter of Martha Washington. Amazingly, Tudor Place was lived in by successive generations of the Peter family from 1805 to 1984. Now a museum, visitors may view its rooms, furnishings, and family memorabilia, which includes some of George Washington's personal possessions (202-965-0400, www. tudor-place.org).

On leaving Tudor Place turn right (south) and walk on 31st Street to Q Street. Turn right onto Q Street and walk west two blocks to Wisconsin Avenue. Wisconsin Avenue and M Street are Georgetown's main thoroughfares. Turn left onto Wisconsin and walk three blocks south. Turn left onto Dumbarton Street and the **Dumbarton United Methodist Church (8)** will be on the left. The yellow brick facade (1894) belies the antebellum church within. Like so many churches, it served as a hospital during the Civil War. Tradition has it that Walt Whitman, who was a nurse as well as a poet, tended the sick and wounded here.

Walk on Dumbarton Street and turn right onto 29th Street and then right again onto N Street. Stop at number 3014, which will be on your left. This is known as the **Laird-Dunlop House (9).** Built in 1799 for the merchant John Laird, the house passed to his daughter Barbara, who wed James Dunlop. Abraham Lincoln's son, Robert Todd Lincoln, bought this house in 1915 and built number 3018 next door.

You will now see the two houses occupied by Jacqueline Bouvier Kennedy and her two children in the days following her husband's assassination in 1963. Walk to number 3038 N Street. This was the **home of Averell and Marie Harriman (10),** who lent their house to the first lady immediately following her husband's death. Mrs. Kennedy lived here for four months until she bought a home of her own, which you will now see.

Backtrack just a few steps to **3017 N Street (11).** After Mrs. Kennedy lived in the Harrimans' house she made what she hoped to be a more permanent move to this house. Unfortunately, the curiosity seekers who literally camped at her front door were a source of concern to Mrs. Kennedy. After only 10 months in this house Jacqueline Kennedy and her children moved to a sprawling apartment high above Fifth Avenue on New York's Upper East Side. This was her final move; she died in her New York apartment on May 19, 1994. An aside: this house was built in the 1700s and was once a female academy.

Resume your walk west on N Street, crossing Wisconsin Avenue. The series of dwellings on the right between Potomac and 33rd Streets is Smith Row. Walter and Clement Smith built this block of Federal rowhouses in 1815.

A third **Kennedy house (12)** is at 3307 N Street. This Federal house was built in 1811, bought by Senator John Kennedy in 1957, and presented to his wife Jacqueline as a gift. She then decorated the house three times in the first year alone. The Kennedys lived here when their children Caroline and John Jr. were born. In 1961 they moved directly from this house to the White House.

Walk along N Street to another row of Federal houses, **Cox Row (13),** at numbers 3327–3339. These were built by Major Cox in 1805; the Marquis de Lafayette was entertained in number 3337.

Continue two more blocks and another landmark associated with the Kennedys will be on the right. **Holy Trinity Church (14)** was founded in 1794, and its present church building was dedicated in 1851. Senator Jack Kennedy and his family often attended mass here.

At the end of N Street turn right onto 37th Street,

Georgetown

and **Georgetown University (15)** will be on the left
(202-687-0100, www.georgetown.edu). Founded in
1789, this is the oldest Roman Catholic college in the
United States. GU is a Jesuit school, but from its incep-
tion it has enrolled people of any faith. To visit campus,
enter at 37th and O Streets. The building before you is
Healy Hall (1879). A statue of the university's founder,
Father John Carroll, stands in the center of the circle in
front of the hall. Note also the two cannons. These were
aboard the ships *Ark* and *Dove* that brought the Jesuits
to Maryland in 1634 (see the tour "St. Mary's City").

Walk through Healy Hall to the **Quadrangle (16),**
which is enclosed by some of the school's older buildings: Old North (1795) to the right, Ryan Hall (1904)
to the left, and Dahlgren Chapel of the Sacred Heart in
between. Some scenes from *The Exorcist* were filmed in
this chapel. The author, Peter Blatty, is a GU alumnus.

On leaving the university look to your left to the

Georgetown Visitation Preparatory School (17), which was founded by cloistered nuns in 1799. The convent, the second oldest in America, suffered a devastating fire in 1993.

Walk down O Street to the **Bodisco House (18)** at number 3322, which was built in 1815. General Robert E. Lee's mother lived here after fleeing Alexandria during the Civil War. Later made the Imperial Russian Embassy, its ambassador, Baron Alexander de Bodisco, aged 62, married Harriet Williams, a Georgetown girl, aged 16. The couple lived happily ever after, hosting many lavish parties at Bodisco House.

Continue on O Street and **St. John's Episcopal Church (19)** will be on the right. Thought by some to be another William Thornton building, the stuccoed, Federal-style church was built between 1796 and 1806. Both Thomas Jefferson and Francis Scott Key attended services here. In the 1830s St. John's was facing a bleak financial future when financier William Wilson Corcoran saved it.

When you reach Wisconsin Avenue turn right and walk to the corner of M Street. **Georgetown Park (20),** an urban mall of shops, restaurants, and eateries, will be in font of you.

Kitty-corner to Georgetown Park is the **Riggs Bank Building (21).** William Wilson Corcoran and George W. Riggs founded a bank in 1840 named, appropriately, Corcoran and Riggs. Corcoran retired, turning his attention to his philanthropies, including the Corcoran Gallery of Art and the Oak Hill Cemetery. This branch of the Riggs Bank was built in 1922 (William J. Marsh and Walter Peter, architects). The gold dome crowning the white marble, classical revival bank has become a landmark here at the intersection of Georgetown's two busiest streets.

Walk east on M Street to **the Old Stone House (22).** Built in 1765, Georgetown's oldest house is now a museum operated by the National Park Service. In addition to period rooms, there are historic exhibits and a lovely garden (202-426-6851, www.nps/gov/rocr/oldstonehouse/).

Next door are two more 18th-century buildings: 3001 and 3003 M Street. These were the property of Thomas Sim Lee, a Maryland governor and a patriot.

From M Street turn right onto Thomas Jefferson Street and walk south one block to the **Chesapeake and Ohio Canal (23).** A delightful footpath parallels the canal. The National Park Service offers leisurely, one-hour excursions on mule-drawn canal boats. Personnel dressed in period costume enhance the experience (202-653-5190, www.np.gov/choh).

Following the ride on the canal, continue south on Thomas Jefferson Street. The **Duvall Foundry Building (24)** will be on the left. Once a hospital for canal mules, it is now an urban mall. Another block south is **Washington Harbor (25),** a mammoth complex of condominiums, offices, shops, and restaurants completed in 1987 and designed by Arthur Cotton Moore. Your walking tour of Georgetown ends here where you may walk along the banks of the Potomac River on the boardwalk, take a river cruise, or simply sit among the sculptures by J. Seward Johnson Jr. (202-944-4242).

6 · Embassy Row and Dupont Circle

Directions: *By car:* From points west or south, take the Capital Beltway to I-66 east to US 50 east (Constitution Avenue). Turn left onto 23rd Street, go around one third of Washington Circle to New Hampshire Avenue (northeast) to Dupont Circle. From points north or east, take I-95 to US 295 to US 50 west (New York Avenue). At Mt. Vernon Square turn right (northwest) onto Massachusetts Avenue to Dupont Circle. *By public transportation:* Take the Metro to the Dupont Circle station (202-637-7000, www.wmata.com).

Pierre L'Enfant planned seven circles for the District. This is the largest. In the late 19th century it developed into one of the city's most desirable neighborhoods. Many of the mansions built in the Gilded Age have become embassies.

Dupont Circle (1) is named for Rear Admiral Samuel Francis Dupont, who fought for the Union during the Civil War. The fountain at the center of the circle is his memorial. It was modeled in 1921 by Daniel Chester French, whose best-known work is the statue at the Lincoln Memorial.

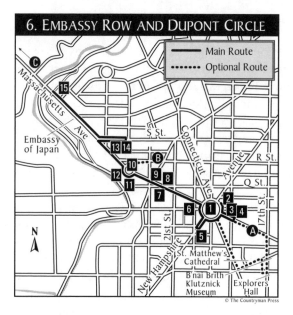

6. EMBASSY ROW AND DUPONT CIRCLE

—— Main Route

••••••• Optional Route

Massachusetts Ave

Embassy of Japan

S St.

Connecticut Ave

R St.

Q St.

17th St.

21st St.

New Hampshire Ave

N

St. Matthew's Cathedral

B'nai Brith Klutznick Museum

Explorers Hall

© The Countryman Press

Looking east, at the corner of P Street, you will see the **Washington Club (2).** It was built in 1903 as the home for the Patterson family. Inspired by 16th-century Italian palazzi, the house was designed by McKim, Mead, and White. In 1927 President and Mrs. Coolidge lived here for a time while work was being done on the White House. Charles Lindbergh, who had completed his transatlantic flight, was a guest of the first family. Large crowds gathered here to see the famed aviator, who on occasion obliged them by appearing on the second-floor balcony. The house is now used as a private club.

Walk south on the circle just one more block to Massachusetts Avenue. Turn left onto Massachusetts Avenue and the **Sulgrave Club (3)** will be on the left at number 1801. Built about 1900 for the Wadsworth family, this is now also a private club.

Continue on Massachusetts Avenue just a few more steps. The headquarters for the **National Trust for Historic Preservation (4)** will be on the left at number 1785, a building known as the McCormick Apartments. Built in 1915 (Jules Henri de Sibour, architect) for the heir to the reaper fortune, this was Washington's most fashionable apartment building. It has belonged to the National Trust since 1997 (202-588-6000, www.nthp. org).

Option A: There are three sites in the neighborhood well worth a 4-block detour. Walk down Massachusetts Avenue to 17th Street and turn right. Then walk south on 17th Street two blocks to Rhode Island Avenue. The B'nai B'rith Klutznick Museum will be on the left. The museum's permanent collection includes over 500 objects, some of them thousands of years old (202-857-6583, www.bnaibrith.org/museum/index.cfm).

Continue south on 17th Street just one more block, and Explorers Hall will be on the left. At the headquarters of the National Geographic Society, the hall contains a museum about the society, its history, its work, and (you guessed it) the world. In fact, the world's largest free-standing globe (over 10 feet in diameter) is here. Changing exhibits are also mounted (202-857-7588, www.nationalgeographic.com).

Retrace your steps on 17th Street north to Rhode Island Avenue. Turn left onto Rhode Island Avenue and St. Matthew's Cathedral will be on the right. The parish was founded in 1840, and this cathedral church was built in 1889 (Heins and LaFarge, architects). A Renaissance Revival design, the cathedral's exterior may be plain and almost fortresslike, but its interior is richly embellished with mosaics, frescoes, and marble. John F. Kennedy's funeral mass took place in St. Matthew's on November 25, 1963, and a marker on the nave floor indicates where his casket was placed for the service (202-347-3215, www.stmatthewscathedral.org).

To return to the main tour, walk on Rhode Island Avenue west to Connecticut Avenue and then north 3 blocks to Dupont Circle.

Return to Dupont Circle. Turn left onto New Hampshire Avenue and the **Historical Society of Washington, D.C. (5)** will be on the left at number 1307, housed in the Christian Heurich Mansion. Heurich was a German immigrant who made his fortune brewing beer. This lavish Romanesque Revival house, complete with turret and porte cochere, was built for him in 1894 (John Granville Myers, architect). The house and its library are open to the public (202-785-2068, www.hswdc.org).

Retrace your steps to Dupont Circle. Walk clockwise past P Street and then turn left onto Massachusetts Avenue. The **Blaine Mansion (6)** will be on the left at number 2000. The house was built in 1881 for Maine senator James G. Blaine. Walk northwest on Massachusetts Avenue and you will see two embassies: Indonesia on the left at number 2020 and India on the right at number 2107.

Stop at the **Anderson House (7),** at number 2118 on the left. It was built in 1902 for diplomat Larz Anderson (Little and Browne, architects), who bequeathed it to the Society of the Cincinnati, whose membership is limited to descendants of Revolutionary War Continental Army and Naval Officers. Step inside. The first floor houses the society's museum of Revolutionary War memorabilia and its library; the second floor is furnished as the Andersons left it (202-785-2040).

Cross Massachusetts Avenue to Q Street and turn right. The **Phillips Collection (8)** will be on the left at the corner of Q and 21st Streets. In 1921, Mr. and Mrs. Duncan Phillips opened their house to the public to show their collection of late-19th-century and 20th-century art. This is said to be the nation's first museum of modern art. A signature piece in the collection is Renoir's *Luncheon of the Boating Party*. Van Gogh, Degas, Manet, Monet, Daumier, Cézanne, Eakins, and O'Keeffe are all represented in the permanent collection of 2,500 works (202-387-2151, www.phillipscollection.org).

Return to Massachusetts Avenue and turn right. The **Cosmos Club (9)** will be on the right at the corner of 22nd Street. The club occupies the Townsend House, which was built in 1895 for railroad executive Robert H. Townsend. The architectural firm, Carrere and Hastings, also designed the New York Public Library. It became a private club in 1950.

Continue to walk northwest on Massachusetts Avenue and the embassies will begin to appear in greater number on both sides of the avenue. They include Luxembourg (number 2200), Togo (2208), Sudan (2210), Greece (2221), Ireland (2234), and South Korea (2320).

At this point you will be at **Sheridan Circle (10),** named for Civil War General William Tecumseh Sherman. A statue depicts the general mounted on his horse Winchester. This was modeled in 1908 by Gutzon Borglum, who is best remembered for his work on Mount Rushmore.

The **Embassy of Turkey (11)** occupies an opulent mansion at 1606 23rd Street. It was built in 1910 for Edward H. Everett, who amassed a vast fortune through his invention, the fluted soft-drink bottle cap. The building's architect was George Oakley Totten, Jr.

The next building to note is the **Alice Pike House and Studio (12)** at 2304 Massachusetts Avenue. The house's collection and furnishings were acquired in 1971 by the Smithsonian's National Museum of American Art. It is not open to the public.

Option B: R Street is a detour with a number of embassies and two museums. The embassies are Egypt (number 2301), Kenya (2249), and the Philippines (2253). The Fonda del Sol Visual Arts Center is at 2112 R Street (near 21st Street). Opened in1973, this is a "bilingual community museum directed by artists and community members dedicated to presenting, promoting, and preserving the cultural heritage and arts of the Americas." Pre-Columbian, folk, and contemporary arts are exhibited and bilingual programs are offered (202-483-2777).

Just a block farther down R Street is the National Museum of American Jewish Military History (1811 R Street). Three floors of galleries document and present the contributions and participation of American Jews in the military. The museum is open under the auspices of the Jewish War Veterans of the USA (202-265-6280, www.penfed.org/ jwv/museum.htm).

To resume the main walking tour, continue up Massachusetts Avenue. Turn right onto S Street; the **Woodrow Wilson House (13)** will be on the right at number 2340. The house was built in 1915; the architect was Waddy Wood. In 1921, President and Mrs. Wilson

Dupont Circle

retired to this house. Interestingly, it is said that Wilson was the only former president to retire to Washington. He lived here just three years until his death in 1924. Mrs. Wilson survived her husband by nearly four decades. She died in 1961. Now owned by the National Trust, the house is opened to the public, who may see this large, comfortable home, which is filled with Wilson memorabilia (202-387-4062, www.nationaltrust. org).

Walk on S Street just a few more steps to the **Textile Museum (14)** at number 2320. The museum is in a house designed by John Russell Pope (architect for the National Galley of Art and the Jefferson Memorial). The Textile Museum was founded in 1925 by George Hewitt Myers. Its collection has grown to include over 16,000 textiles dating from 3000 B.C. to the present. In addition to the galleries, the museum also includes the Arthur D. Jenkins Library (202-667-0441, www.textilemuseum. org).

Return to Massachusetts Avenue. Turn right onto the avenue and the Venezuelan Embassy will be on the right at numbers 2443–2445. Just a few steps away, on the opposite side of Massachusetts Avenue, you'll see the Japanese Embassy at number 2520. The Georgian Revival building was finished in 1931; a second building (on the right) was completed in 1986.

This walking tour ends at the **Islamic Center (15)** at 2551 Massachusetts Avenue. You will easily recognize the mosque as you approach it, its 160-foot-tall minaret towering over its neighbors. Built between 1949 and 1957, this was one of the first mosques in the United States. Step inside. Following Islamic custom, you will have to leave your shoes by the door and have your arms and legs modestly covered. Women must cover their heads. The mosque's interior is richly embellished with mosaics, Turkish tiles, Persian carpets, and a large Egyptian chandelier. A library and gift shop are also at the mosque (202-332-3451).

The main tour ends here. To return to Dupont Circle, take the N2, N4, or N6 bus down Massachusetts Avenue.

Option C: For the hearty walker this option continues up Massachusetts Avenue about a mile farther. Should you take this option, you will be rewarded with seeing more embassies, an observatory, the vice president's house, and two cathedrals.

Cross Rock Creek Park on the Charles Glover Bridge, built in 1940. Mr. Glover was a philanthopist and a financier. The buildings of the Brazilian Embassy will be on the left. One of them, an Italian Renaissance palazzo at number 3000, was designed by John Russell Pope in 1909. Its more modern neighbor at number 3006 was designed in 1971 by Brazilian architect Olavo Redig de Campos.

Continue up Massachusetts Avenue. The Bolivian Embassy is at numbers 3012–3014. A memorial garden dedicated to Lebanese-American philosopher and poet Kahlil Gibran will be on the left between 30th and 34th Streets and provides a good place to rest a bit.

Look for the statue of Winston Churchill on the left, marking your approach to the British Embassy. The statue was thoughtfully placed here in 1966, with the prime minister's right foot on American soil and his left on the embassy property. Resembling an elegant British country estate, the embassy and the ambassador's residence (in the right wing) were built in 1931 (Sir Edwin Lutyens, architect).

As you continue up Massachusetts Avenue you will find yourself following Observatory Circle in a counterclockwise direction. The U.S. Naval Observatory is on the left (202-762-1468, www.usno.navy.mil). The observatory is open to visitors on Monday evenings; it is advisable to call in advance. The observatory property is adjacent to the vice president's house. Built in 1891 for the observatory's superintendent, in 1974 it was officially delegated to the vice president. It is not open to the public.

As you walk farther on Massachusetts Avenue, the Greek Orthodox Saint Sophia Cathedral will be on the right at 36th Street. Built in 1956 and designed by Archie Protopapas, the interior features stunning mosaics by Demetrios Dukas.

Turn right onto Wisconsin Avenue and Washington National Cathedral will be on the right. Officially named the Cathedral Church of St. Peter and St. Paul, this is the seat for the Episcopal Diocese of Washington. Though not in any way affiliated with the federal government, the cathedral is the site of many services, celebrations, and funerals. Building the cathedral was a massive undertaking that spanned most of the 20th century. The cornerstone was laid in 1907, and the dedication of the completed church took place in 1990. Through the long process, the cathedral has had about a dozen architects. Based on 14th-century Gothic prototypes, this is the sixth largest church in the world, and the second largest in the nation (New York's Cathedral of St. John the Divine is bigger). You may take the elevator up into the west tower for a bird's-eye view of the city. Walk down the nave and study the stained-glass windows. The Space Window is embedded with a rock from the moon. Visit the Children's Chapel, which is built and furnished to scale for little ones. The crypt is the oldest part of the cathedral, and it is where Woodrow Wilson is interred. Interestingly, he is one of three American presidents who have their final resting place in a church. John Adams and John Quincy Adams, entombed in Quincy, Massachusetts, are the other two. There is a gift shop in the crypt, and tours are given. Visit the gardens, some of which were designed by Frederick Law Olmsted (202-537-6200, www.cathedral.org/cathedral).

There is no Metro stop here. However, the N2, N4, and N6 buses will bring you back down Massachusetts Avenue, retracing the route to the Dupont Circle station.

II. Virginia

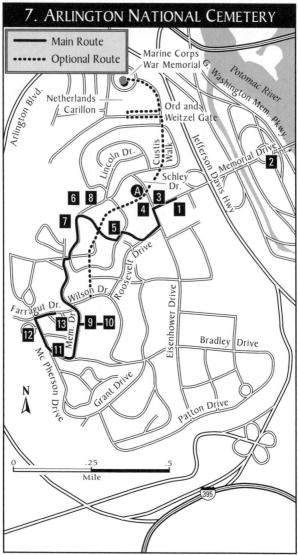

7. ARLINGTON NATIONAL CEMETERY

— Main Route
···· Optional Route

Marine Corps
War Memorial

Potomac River

G. Washington Mem. Pkwy

Netherlands
Carillon

Ord and
Weitzel Gate

Arlington Blvd.

Lincoln Dr.

Custis Walk

Schley Dr.

Jefferson Davis Hwy

Memorial Drive

2

A

6 **8**

7

5

4 **3**

1

Roosevelt Drive

Wilson Dr.

Eisenhower Drive

Bradley Drive

Farragut Dr.

Mem. Dr.

13

9 **10**

12

11

Mc Pherson Drive

Grant Drive

Patton Drive

N

0   .25   .5
Mile

395

© The Countryman Press

7 · Arlington National Cemetery

Directions: *By car:* From the Capital Beltway take I-66 east to Arlington. *By public transportation:* Take the Metro to the Arlington Cemetery stop (202-637-7000, www.wmata.com).

Arlington National Cemetery, covering over 600 acres, contains more than 210,000 graves, including those of soldier heroes from every American conflict from the Revolution to the present. The entire cemetery was once a part of the Arlington House estate, which is a stop on this walk. Built in 1818 for George Washington Parke Custis (Martha Washington's grandson by her first marriage) the house and estate passed to his daughter, Mary Anna, who married Robert E. Lee. The Lees left Arlington House in 1861, he to assume command of Virginia's Confederate forces, and she for reasons of security and safety. The couple never returned. It was seized by the federal government and used as an outpost overlooking the Potomac River during the Civil War. The first burial here (that of a Union soldier) took place in 1864 and in 1883 the estate was officially designated a national cemetery.

Begin at the **visitors center (1)** (703-697-2131,

www.arlingtoncemetery.com). When leaving the center
look to your right for a view of the **Arlington Memorial Bridge (2).** Built in 1920 as a ceremonial route
from the Lincoln Memorial, it was inspired by the Ponte
Sant' Angelo, which spans the Tiber River in Rome. The
monumental gilded equestrian statues that guard the
bridge at either end were gifts from Italy.

After looking at the bridge, turn left and approach
the cemetery, passing the **Memorial Gate (3),** designed
by McKim, Mead, and White in 1926. Note Arlington
House on top of the hill. Below the house and directly
in front of you is the Hemicycle, built in 1932. The
Hemicycle is now the entranceway to the **Memorial
Dedicated to Women in Military Service for America (4).** Completed in 1997 according to designs by
Marion Gail Weiss and Michael A. Manfredi, this is the
nation's first major memorial dedicated to the nearly
two million women who have served in the armed
forces. Step inside to the Hall of Honor, exhibit gallery,
theater, and shop. The upper terrace has panoramic
views of the cemetery and the city (703-533-1155, 1-
800-222-2294, www.womensmemorial.org).

As you leave the memorial turn right and then make
a second right at the next corner. This will lead you to
President John F. Kennedy's grave (5). The site was
chosen by his widow, because she knew this was one
of the president's favorite spots. He would often come
here, pause, and enjoy the view of the capital. The Eter-
nal Flame has been burning since Mrs. Kennedy lit it on
the day of his burial, November 25, 1963. Her grave,
just a few feet away, is inscribed JACQUELINE BOUVIER
KENNEDY ONASSIS. Two of the couple's children (a still-
born child and Patrick, who lived for just 38 hours in

1963) are also buried here, alongside their parents. Look for the white cross nearby which marks the grave of Senator Robert F. Kennedy, who was slain by an assassin's bullet on June 6, 1968.

Follow the path to **Arlington House (6),** built in 1818, a splendid early example of Greek Revival design. Its architect was the Englishman George Hadfield. It has been said that this house inspired the use of Greek Revival design in so many of Washington's public buildings. In 1883 the U.S. Supreme Court ruled that the house and the estate should be returned to the Lee family. By that time Robert E. Lee and his wife had not lived in the house for more than 20 years, a federal cemetery containing more than 16,000 graves was in their garden, and Lee had a home in Lexington, Virginia, where he was president of Washington and Lee University (see "Lexington"). In lieu of repossessing their estate the Lees were compensated $150,000. Also known as the Robert E. Lee Memorial, Arlington House is open to the public by the National Park Service (703-557-0613, www.nps.gov/arho/). A walk through the garden will lead you to the old **Amphitheater and Rostrum (7),** and it will also lead you to the Tomb of the Unknown Civil War Dead.

Between Arlington House and the city you'll see **Pierre L'Enfant's grave (8).** L'Enfant (1754–1825) designed the street pattern for Washington. Unfortunately, he was never given recognition or proper compensation for his work. At first buried in an obscure site outside the city, his remains were moved to this site in 1909 by the Daughters of the American Revolution, overlooking the city and his work.

From Arlington House, turn to face the city and take

the road on the right to Meigs Drive. Turn right onto Meigs Drive and then left onto Memorial Drive. Walk a short distance and **Memorial Amphitheater (9)** will be on the left. This structure was built in 1915–1921 to replace the first, smaller amphitheater seen on this walk. Dominating the amphitheater are words taken from Lincoln's Gettysburg Address: "We here highly resolve that these dead shall not have died in vain."

Behind the Amphitheater is the **Tomb of the Unknowns (10),** first dedicated in 1926 as a resting place for a soldier slain in World War I. Nearby crypts today also contain the remains of unknown soldiers from World War II and Korea. The remains of a soldier killed in the Vietnam War were interred here until they were identified through DNA testing and then returned to his family. The guards at the tombs are on duty 24 hours a day. The changing of the guard takes place every half-hour April through September, and hourly the rest of the year.

Return to Memorial Drive, turn left, and then turn right onto Porter Drive. The **Nurse's Memorial (11)** will be on the right. Porter Drive leads into McPherson Drive. The memorial to Theodore Roosevelt's Spanish-American War Rough Riders will be on the right and, just beyond that the **Confederate Monument (12)** is on the left. Dedicated in 1914, the monument is encircled by the graves of nearly 500 Confederate soldiers whose bodies were moved here from several other locations.

Continue on McPherson Drive a few more steps, and then turn right onto Farragut Drive. On the left you'll see the **mast from the U.S.S.** *Maine* **(13).** The *Maine* was destroyed by a Spanish mine in 1898, killing 266 on board and igniting the Spanish-American War. Next

Arlington National Cemetery

to the mast, closer to Farragut Drive, is the grave of Ignace Paderewski, a Polish pianist, composer, and prime minister. Exiled from his country during World War II, he died in 1941.

Walk to the end of Farragut Drive. Jog to the left onto Memorial Drive, and then turn right onto Wilson Drive. At the **T** turn left onto Roosevelt Drive, which will lead you back to Memorial Drive and the cemetery's entrance.

Option A: The grave of William Howard Taft (1857–1930) is on the left on Schley Drive beyond the Memorial to Women in Military Service. The Custis Walk, beginning at Wilson Drive, is an alternate route to Taft's grave. Taft was our 27th president (1909–1913) and later the tenth chief justice of the Supreme Court (1921–1930).

From President Taft's grave follow the Custis Walk to the Ord and Weitzel Gate. The Netherlands Carillon will be on your left. The carillon has 49 bells, each the gift of a group of Dutch citizens. The carillon was a thank-you gift for the help extended by the United States government and its people during World War II and the years following. For concert schedule call 703-

289-2530. Just a few steps away is the Marine Corps War Memorial, also known as the Iwo Jima Statue. The inspiration for the statue was a photo taken by Joseph Rosenthal, which captures forever the image of five marines and one sailor raising the flag on Mount Suribachi after a brutal World War II battle. Sculptor Felix de Weldon modeled this, the largest bronze statue ever cast. It is 78 feet long and weighs 100 tons.

Those using public transportation may retrace their steps to the Arlington Cemetery Metro stop or, as an alternative, walk north from the statue three blocks on Meade Street to the Rosslyn Metro station.

8 · Alexandria

Directions: *By car:* From Washington take the 14th Street bridge (US 1 south) to Alexandria. In Alexandria US 1 becomes Henry Street. Turn left onto King Street, drive for two blocks, and turn right onto Alfred Street. The Friendship Fire House will be on the right. *By public transportation:* Take the Metro to the King Street stop (202-637-7000, www.wmata.com). Walk nine blocks east on King Street or take the DASH shuttle to King and Alfred Streets. *Note:* Option A visits the George Washington Masonic National Memorial, which is next to the King Street stop. If you are using the Metro and you wish to visit the memorial, you may want to do this before beginning the main tour.

As early as 1695 Europeans settled in this area, which was then known as Belhaven. By the mid-18th century many Scottish merchants made this port on the Potomac River their home. Alexandria was founded in 1749 and named for John Alexander, a Scottish landowner and merchant. George Washington lived here and helped create the town's street plan. Later, Washington proposed that Alexandria be part of the capital. When the District of Columbia was planned in

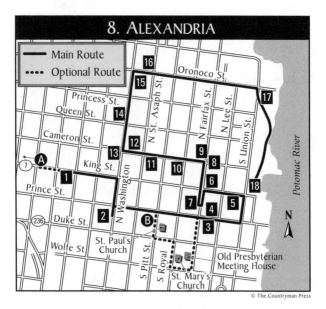

© The Countryman Press

the 1790s, a city 10 miles square was envisioned, with land ceded from Maryland and Virginia on both sides of the Potomac River. The donation was not permanent. In 1847, Alexandria reverted to the Commonwealth of Virginia. Occupied by Union troops during the Civil War, the city was spared many of the war's hostilities. Alexandria always has been, and remains, a quiet residential community just 8 miles down the Potomac River from the capital. Many of its old homes and charming, tree-lined streets have been lovingly preserved.

This tour of Old Town Alexandria begins at the **Friendship Fire House (1),** at 107 South Alfred Street, near King Street. Founded in 1774, the Friendship Fire Company was Alexandria's first volunteer fire company.

One member was townsman George Washington, who presented the company with its first fire engine in 1775. This and many other pieces of fire-fighting equipment are on display at the museum. The present firehouse was built in 1855 and restored in 1992. The weather vane on the cupola is in fact the company's emblem (703-838-3891).

Option A: Nine blocks west on King Street is the George Washington Masonic National Memorial. Set on Shuter's Hill, this site was favored by Thomas Jefferson for the national capitol. It was used as a Union encampment during the Civil War. In 1923 the cornerstone was laid for this, the Masons' memorial to one of their most famous members. The model for the memorial was the ancient lighthouse that stood in Alexandria, Egypt. Enter the monument to visit its museum, which includes artifacts that belonged to George Washington. An elevator provides access to the observation level (703-683-2007, www.gwmemorial.org).

Walk east on King Street, away from the monument and toward the river. Turn right onto South Washington Street. The Confederate Monument (1889) will be at the corner of Washington and Prince Streets. At 201 South Washington Street you'll see the **Lyceum (2)** on the right. This, Alexandria's historical museum, occupies a Greek Revival building designed by Benjamin Howell in 1839. Step inside. The Lyceum's permanent and changing exhibits provide an excellent introduction to the town and its history (703-838-4994, www.pha.ci. alexandria.va.us/lyceum/).

After visiting the Lyceum walk east on Prince Street to Fairfax Street.

Option B: Three historic churches, each built for a

different denomination, are just off Prince Street. To see them, turn right onto South Pitt Street. St. Paul's Episcopal Church will be on the left. Designed in 1818 by one of America's leading architects, Benjamin Latrobe, its interior is reminiscent of Sir Christopher Wren's St. James Church in Piccadilly, London. Its congregation was not sympathetic to the Union cause during the Civil War, and the church was seized by Federal troops and put to use as a hospital (703-549-3312, www.st-paulsepis.com/).

Turn left from St. Paul's to Duke Street. Then turn left onto Duke Street and right onto South Royal Street. St. Mary's Church will be on the left. Founded in 1793, this was the first Roman Catholic congregation in Virginia. Tradition has it that George Washington, though an Episcopalian, made a donation to the building fund for the first church building, which has since been demolished. The present church was built in 1826 and enlarged in 1888 (703-548-6833).

On leaving St. Mary's go around the block by turning left onto South Royal Street, left again onto Wolfe Street, and then left onto South Fairfax Street. The Old Presbyterian Meeting House will be on the left. "Resilient" aptly describes this church. It was built in 1775, but destroyed by fire in 1835 after being struck by lightning. Rebuilt using the shell of the first church, it was closed from 1889 to 1949 because its membership had decreased. Reopened and restored, the Meeting House now welcomes visitors (703-549-5570, www.opmh.org). To resume the main tour, turn left from the door of the Meeting House and walk 1½ blocks to Prince Street and turn right.

The **200 block of Prince Street (3),** between South

Fairfax and South Lee, is known as Gentry Row. Number 207 was built for the Fairfax family, and numbers 209 and 211 were homes to physicians who attended George Washington: Dr. James Craik and Dr. Elisha Cullen Dick. Dr. Dick was with Washington when he died, and he stopped the clock in the room at that moment. The clock may be seen at the George Washington Masonic National Memorial (see option A , above). The salmon-colored Greek Revival building at the corner of Prince and Lee is the **Athenaeum (4).** Built in 1859, this was originally the Bank of the Old Dominion. The Athenaeum offers special exhibits and programs and is open to the public (703-548-0035).

Continue to walk east on Prince Street. The 100 block is a charming cobblestone street lined with Federal period houses. The land in this area was owned by Captain John Harper, and for this reason this has become known as Captain's Row.

Turn left onto Union Street and then left onto King Street. The **Corn Exchange Building (5),** at 100 King Street, was built in the 1800s, modeled after Rome's 16th-century Palazzo Farnese.

Visit the **Ramsey House (6)** at 221 King Street. This is believed to be the oldest house in Alexandria. Built in 1724, through its long history it has been a tavern, a rooming house, a grocery store, and a cigar factory. Restored in 1956, it is now the city's visitors center (703-838-4200, www.cybis.com/alex/ramsey.htm).

Walk west to South Fairfax Street. Jog to the left to the **Stabler-Leadbeater Apothecary Shop (7),** at 105–107 South Fairfax. Opened in 1793, this apothecary was frequented by George and Martha Washington and, later, by Robert E. Lee. It was open for business as recently as 1933. Restored, visitors may tour the museum, which includes more than 8,000 artifacts (703-836-3713, www.cybis.com/alex/stabler.htm).

On leaving the apothecary turn left, cross King Street, and walk to the **Carlyle House (8),** at 121 North Fairfax Street. Mimicking the early Georgian Scottish manor house Craigiehall, Carlyle House was built in 1751 for Scottish merchant John Carlyle. British General Edward Braddock made this, Alexandria's first Colonial mansion, his Revolutionary War headquarters. Now restored, Carlyle House is open to visitors. Tours include not only the elegant public rooms but also the family's bedrooms, the slave quarters, and an Architectural Room, which documents and illustrates the house's history. A walk (or rest) in the terraced gardens completes the visit (703-549-2997, www.cybis.com/alex/carlyle.htm).

On leaving Carlyle House walk north on North Fairfax Street. The **Bank of Alexandria (9)** is next door at number 133. The bank was founded in 1792; George Washington was an original shareholder. The building was completed in 1807 and has also served as a hotel and as a Civil War hospital. Just across Cameron Street, at 201 North Fairfax Street, is the Ann Lee Memorial Home, in which Robert E. Lee's mother lived.

Walk west on Cameron Street. City Hall (1873) will be on the left. Stop at **Gadsby's Tavern Museum (10),** 134 North Royal Street, at the corner of Cameron. Actually two buildings, the tavern (a Georgian building) dates to 1770, the city hotel (Federal) dates to 1792. John Gadsby was the proprietor from 1796 to 1808. A main stagecoach stop on the busy route from New England to points south, the tavern and hotel hosted many notables, including George Washington, the Marquis de

Historic homes in Old Town

Lafayette, Thomas Jefferson, John Adams, James Monroe, and Robert E. Lee. Restored in 1976, the museum features the Public Tap Room, Assembly Room, ballroom, and bed chambers (703-838-4242, www.oha.ci. alexandria.va.us/gadsby/).

Resume your walk west on Cameron Street and stop at number 508. A reconstruction, this replicates **George**

Washington's Townhouse (11). This was Washington's in-town quarters when weather or schedule prevented him from making the trek to Mount Vernon.

In the next block the **Yeaton-Fairfax House (12)** stands at 607 Cameron Street. A New Hampshire shipbuilder, William Yeaton moved to Alexandria and built this house in 1803. Yeaton is best known as the designer and builder of Washington's tomb at Mount Vernon.

Walk west one more block on Cameron Street to **Christ Church (13),** 118 North Washington Street. The redbrick wall surrounding the churchyard makes this a quiet haven in Old Town. Pass through the gate and enter the building. John Alexander, for whom Alexandria is named, donated the land for this Episcopal church. It was designed by James Wren, who was related to the famous London architect Sir Christopher Wren. Begun in 1767, construction of the brick and stone church was completed in 1773 by John Carlyle, whose house was described earlier on this tour. The interior gallery was added in 1787, and the pepper pot steeple was added in 1818. George Washington was a vestryman here and sat in pew number 60. Robert E. Lee was confirmed here and sat in pew 46 (703-549-1450, www.historicchristchurch.org).

On leaving Christ Church turn left and walk north on North Washington Street. **Lloyd House (14)** will be on the left at number 220. Built in 1798, this Federal-style house now holds the historical and genealogical collection of the Alexandria Library System (703-838-4577, www.cybis.com/alex/lloyd.htm).

Resume your walk on North Washington Street and stop at the **Lee-Fendell House Museum (15).** Built in 1785, this house was remodeled to the then-popular

Greek Revival style in 1850. From 1785 to 1903 nearly forty Lee family members lived here. George and Martha Washington were dinner guests many times, and General Robert E. Lee visited his cousins on numerous occasions. Now a museum, the Lee-Fendell House has a large collection of Lee family furnishings and memorabilia (703-548-1789).

From North Washington Street turn right (east) onto Oronoco Street. You will pass the **boyhood home of Robert E. Lee (16)** at number 607. The house was built about 1795. In 1810 Robert E. Lee's family moved here from Stratford Hall; he was five years old. In 1825 he left home to study at West Point. The house was a museum for some years, but is currently a private home and not opened to the public.

Continue east on Oronoco Street. Just before the river turn right onto North Union Street and enter **Founder's Park (17).** Walk south through the park, parallel to the riverbank. Return to North Union Street and visit the **Torpedo Factory Art Center (18)** at number 105. Built in 1918, the factory manufactured thousands of torpedoes and other munitions through World War II. After the war it became a storage facility for a myriad of things. In 1974 it opened its doors as an art center (703-838-4565, www.torpedofactory.org). The Torpedo Factory also houses the Alexandria Archaeology Museum. Exhibits tell the story of the colonial town and display the discoveries from recent excavations. Visitors may observe archeologists at work in the museum's laboratory (703-838-4399, www.oha.ci. alexandria.va/us/ archeology/).

This walking tour ends here, on the foot of King Street, with its many shops and eateries. For those using public transportation, there are DASH buses that run straight up King Street to the King Street Metro station.

Also Nearby

Mount Vernon (703-780-2000)

Woodlawn Plantation (703-780-4000)

Gunston Hall Plantation (703-550-9220)

Pohick Church (703-550-9449)

9 · Leesburg

Directions: *By car:* From the Capital Beltway take VA 7 (the Leesburg Pike) north. Turn left onto King Street to the public parking garage. *By public transportation:* Greyhound (1-800-231-2222, www.greyhound.com) has bus service to Leesburg.

In his youth George Washington was a surveyor, and it is known that he mapped this area before Loudoun County was established in 1757. The county was named for the Earl of Loudoun in Scotland, John Campbell, the commander-in-chief of the British forces in North America; the county seat, Leesburg, was named in honor of the Lees, a very influential colonial Virginian family.

Your first stop will be the **Loudoun Museum (1).** Its shop is housed in a cabin built in 1763 and once the place of business for a silversmith. Pause to visit the museum's garden and tour the museum, which is a treasure trove of local memorabilia: over 5,000 artifacts including silver, furniture, documents, letters, textiles, and Civil War items (703-777-7427, www.loudounmuseum.org).

When you leave the museum turn left onto Loudoun Street and left again onto King Street. Cross Market Street and visit the **courthouse (2),** on your right. A

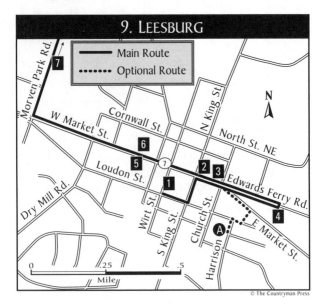

redbrick structure with white Corinthian columns and crowned with a clock and belfry, the courthouse was completed in 1894, replacing an earlier 1811 building. The statue of a Confederate soldier was dedicated in 1908.

Return to Market Street, turn left, and walk east. The columned portico of **Leesburg Academy (3)** will be on the left. Dating to 1848, the academy was a private school for boys. Next, at the corner of Church Street, is the Old Valley Bank Building (1817).

You will come to a fork in the road. Continue straight onto Edwards Ferry Road. On the right will be the entrance to the **George C. Marshall International Center at Dodona Manor (4).** Born in 1901, George Catlett Marshall graduated from the Virginia Military

Institute in 1901 and had a distinguished career as chief of staff of the army (1939–45), secretary of state (1947–49), and, during the Korean War, secretary of defense. He is probably best remembered for the Marshall Plan. He was the first professional soldier to be awarded the Nobel Peace Prize. (The Marshall Memorial Museum and Library is a stop on the Lexington, Virginia walking tour in this guide.) Mrs. Katherine Marshall purchased Dodona Manor to be the family home as well as a retreat. The general retired in 1953 and died in 1959. Undergoing restoration work as this book goes to press, Dodona Manor will be open to the public (703-777-1880, www.georgecmarshall.org).

Retrace your steps along Edwards Ferry Road.

Option A: The Market Station, a collection of unique shops and eateries, is just 2 blocks away. When Edwards Ferry Road meets Market Street, make a hairpin turn to the left onto Market Street. Walking southeast, turn right onto Harrison Street. Market Station will be across Loudoun Street at the next corner.

To continue the tour return to Market Street and walk west, retracing your steps to the courthouse. Pass the courthouse, cross Wirt Street, and the **Presbyterian Church (5),** built in 1804, will be on the left. Opposite the church is the **Thomas Balch Library (6).** Owned and operated by the town, this is a special library for local history and genealogy (703-737-7195, www.leesburgva.org).

The next and final stop on this tour is **Morven Park (7).** It is about a mile from this point, so you may want to consider driving or bicycling to the estate. Continue on Market Street (VA 7), heading west. Turn right onto Morven Park Road and follow the signs to the park.

General Marshall's Dodona Manor

A magnificent 1,200-acre estate, Morven Park's Greek Revival mansion appears to be the quintessential southern plantation. Home to Governor and Mrs. Westmoreland Davis from 1903 to 1954, the house is furnished with their eclectic collection: Flemish tapestries, antique furniture, silver, and artwork. The estate also houses the Museum of Hounds and Hunting; the Winmill Collection of horse-drawn vehicles, livery, harness, and tack; and the Marguerite G. Davis Boxwood Gardens. Special events are held throughout the year (703-777-2414, www.pcthree\loudoun\morvenpark).

Also Nearby

Oatlands (703-777-3173, www.oatlands.org)
National Sporting Museum (504-687-8540, ww.nsl.org)

10 · Winchester

Directions: *By car:* From the Capital Beltway take VA 7 to downtown Winchester. *By public transportation:* Greyhound (1-800-231-2222, www.greyhound.com) has bus service to Winchester.

Before the arrival of English settlers there was a Shawnee village on this site. In 1744 the town was founded by Col. James Wood on land that was owned by Thomas, Lord Fairfax. At first named Fredericktown, in 1752 it was renamed after an English city. George Washington had an office here, which he used first as a surveyor and later as general. Stonewall Jackson and Philip Sheridan, Confederate and Union generals, also had headquarters in Winchester. Notable people born in the town include the explorer Admiral Richard Byrd, author Willa Cather, and singer Patsy Cline.

Begin your tour at the heart of downtown Winchester at the **corner of Braddock and Amherst Street (1).** Facing the parking area, turn left and walk north on Braddock. Note number 103, which was built in 1790. When you reach the next corner, Piccadilly and Braddock, the **Handley Regional Library (2)** will be ahead of you on the left. The library is named for its donor, Judge John Handley, who endowed the city with $2 million for a high school and this library. Remarkably,

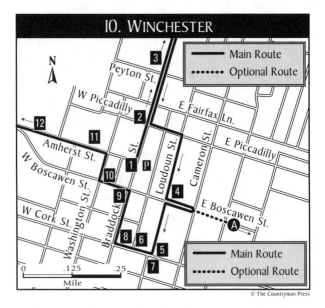

10. WINCHESTER

— Main Route
······ Optional Route

— Main Route
······ Optional Route

© The Countryman Press

Judge Handley was not a Winchester citizen; he lived in Scranton, Pennsylvania. The library's architects were Henry Otis-Chapman and Stewart Barney. Completed in 1913, it has recently been renovated. Note the copper dome that crowns this outstanding example of beaux arts architecture. Step inside. The 3-story rotunda is lit by a stained-glass dome. Many interior details have been carefully preserved, including the original woodwork, lighting fixtures, and the glass floor in the stacks. The Handley's archive room is open to visitors (540-662-9041, www.hrl.lib.state.va.us).

Continue north on Braddock Street. **Stonewall Jackson's headquarters (3)** will be on the left at number 45. This Gothic Revival house was built in 1854, owned by Confederate Col. Lewis T. Moore, and used by Jackson while in Winchester. The house is opened to the public by the Winchester-Frederick County Historical Society (540-667-3242, www.winchesterhistory.org).

Reverse direction and return to Piccadilly Street. Turn left onto Piccadilly and the Old Post Office Building will be on the left. Opposite the post office is a late-18th-century house at number 35.

Turn right onto Loudoun Street and walk down the mall. Note the late 19th-century retail stores on the right. Stop at the **Old Court House Civil War Museum (4)** on the left at 20 South Loudoun Street, just beyond Rouss Street. The first courthouse to stand on this site was built in 1751. This Greek Revival building was completed in 1840 and was used as a prison and a hospital during the Civil War. The museum opened in May 2003 (540-542-1145).

Continue along Loudoun Street; the next corner is Boscawen Street. Turn left onto Boscawen and Rouss City Hall will be on the left at the corner of Cameron Street. Named for its donor, Charles B. Rouss, the Romanesque Revival city hall was built in 1900. The Kurtz Building opposite at 2 Cameron Street was built in 1836 and is now a cultural center.

Option A: If you continue down Boscawen about an eighth of a mile you will arrive at the gate of Mount Hebron Cemetery at East Lane, dating to the 18th century. Many Revolutionary War soldiers are buried here. Gen. Daniel Morgan—Winchester resident, Revolutionary War hero, and congressman—is buried here. Facing the cemetery gate at East Lane turn left, and the ruins of the Old Lutheran Church (1764) will be on the right. Farther along East Lane the Old Stone Presbyterian Church (1788) will also be on the right. Retrace your steps along East Lane, turn left onto Woodstock Lane, and the Confederate Monument will be on the right in Stonewall Cemetery. Opposite, to the left on Woodstock Lane, is the National Cemetery.

Resuming the main tour at city hall, return to Loudoun Street, turn left, and walk south on Loudoun. You will be walking by several late-18th-century dwellings at numbers 2, 4, 21, 28, and 39. The Gothic Revival church on the left is the **First Presbyterian Church (5),** built in 1841. Opposite the church is a more recent addition to Winchester: the **Shenandoah Valley Discovery Museum (6),** at 54 South Loudoun Street. A hands-on learning center for children, the museum includes nine exhibits focusing on the arts and sciences, mathematics, and the humanities (540-722-2020, www.discoverymuseum.net).

At the corner of Loudoun and Cork Streets, the **Red Lion Tavern (7),** circa 1790, will be kitty-corner to the left—the southeast corner.

George Washington's Office Museum (8) will be on the right at 32 West Cork Street. It was built about 1748; George Washington used this log and stone house in 1753 while he supervised the construction of Fort Loudoun. The cabin is open to the public by the Winchester-Frederick County Historical Society (540-662-4412, www.winchesterhistory.org).

Turn right onto Braddock Street, walk two blocks, and then turn left onto Boscawen Street. The **Rouss Fire Hall (9),** constructed in 1896, will be on the corner to the left. Like the city hall, this is another Romanesque Revival building donated by Charles B. Rouss, a wealthy merchant. Note the fireman on the weather vane that, fittingly, crowns the fire hall.

The Handley Library in 1914

The house at 125 West Boscawen Street was built about 1815. Opposite the house is the Gothic Revival **Christ Episcopal Church (10),** completed in 1828. Lord Fairfax is buried in the churchyard. He lived to be 89 and died in 1781.

Turn right onto Washington Street and walk one block to the corner of Amherst Street. Turn left. **Gen. Daniel Morgan's house (11)** will be on the right at 226 Amherst Street. The house was built in 1786. After the American Revolution, General Morgan served in Congress, died in 1802, and was buried in the Mount Hebron Cemetery.

The final stop on this tour is **Glen Burnie (12),** which is just about a mile down Amherst Street. It is a pleasant walk through a neighborhood of large old houses. Should you wish to drive to Glen Burnie, the parking area and starting point for this tour is just one block to the east, where Amherst Street ends at Braddock Street.

Glen Burnie was the home of Col. James Wood, who founded Winchester in 1744. His descendants lived in this house for over 200 years. Now the house, filled with family memorabilia, antique furnishings, and artwork, is open to the public. Visitors are also welcome to explore the 25-acre garden, which is divided into several areas: the rose, pattern, perennial, herb, vegetable, water, and Chinese gardens (540-662-1473, www.glen-burniemuseum.org).

Also Nearby

Abraham's Delight Museum (1754) / Winchester-Frederick County Historical Society (540-662-6519, www.winchesterhistory.org

Patsy Cline Gravesite and Memorial, US 522 south (enter through the north gate and take first right to a bench on left).

Belle Grove Plantation (540-869-2028)

II · Fredericksburg

Directions: *By car:* Take I-95 south to exit 130A (US 3). Follow the signs to US 3 east Business/Downtown (William Street). From William Street turn right onto Princess Anne Street. Drive three blocks and turn left onto Charlotte Street. The visitors center will be on your left near the corner of Charlotte and Caroline Streets. *By public transportation:* Both Amtrak (1-800-USA-RAIL, www.amtrak.com) and Greyhound (1-800-231-2222, www.greyhound.com) serve Fredericksburg.

Set along the banks of the Rappahannock River, this area was first settled in 1671. In 1727 the town's streets were laid, and the place was named in honor of Prince Frederick Louis, father of England's King George III. The town's busy port exported tobacco and grain, and was the port of entry for goods from Europe. For many Fredericksburg is closely associated with George Washington. As a boy he lived on Ferry Farm in the surrounding countryside, and tradition has it that here George cut down the legendary cherry tree. George Washington's mother, his sister Betty, and his brother Charles had homes in Fredericksburg, all of which you will see on this tour. A strategic point during the Civil War, Fredericksburg was alternately controlled by

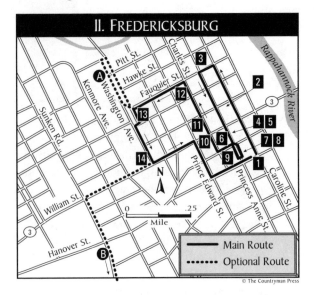

Union and Confederate forces seven times. Four major battles were fought here: Fredericksburg, Chancellorsville, Wilderness, and Spotsylvania. This walk highlights sites from both the Colonial and the Civil War eras.

Begin your tour of Fredericksburg National Historic District at the **Visitors Center (1)** at 706 Caroline Street near Hanover Street (540-373-1776, 1-800-678-4748, www.fredericksburgvirginia.net). Tickets for six sites on this tour are for sale at the visitors center and at the sites themselves. Or you may purchase discounted combination tickets. The sites are: the Hugh Mercer Apothecary Shop, the James Monroe Museum, the Mary Washington House, Kenmore, Rising Sun Tavern, and the Fredericksburg Area Museum and Cultural Center.

With your back to the visitors center turn left and begin walking up Caroline Street. Your first stop will be the **Hugh Mercer Apothecary Shop (2),** on the left, at 1020 Caroline. Dr. Hugh Mercer joined the Continental Army in 1776, achieving the rank of Brigadier General. His shop has been restored and is well stocked with 18th-century remedies and medicines. Costumed interpreters are on hand to give presentations and answer your questions. The apothecary includes an 18th-century medicinal herb garden (540-373-3362). General Mercer was killed at the Battle of Princeton, and you will see his monument later on this tour. An interesting aside: One of his descendants was also a general—George S. Patton.

On leaving the apothecary continue your stroll up lovely Caroline Street. Stop at the **Rising Sun Tavern (3)** at number 1304. This was built in 1760 as a house for Charles Washington, George's brother. In 1792 it became a tavern. Now restored and open to the public, tavern wenches give lively and entertaining tours while serving spiced tea (504-371-1494, 1-800-676-4748).

From the tavern turn right onto Fauquier Street and then left onto Princess Anne Street. Walk south, passing William Street. The **Fredericksburg Area Museum and Cultural Center (4)** will be on the left at number 907. The museum occupies the old town hall and market house. Built in 1816, it is one of the nation's oldest town halls and one of the few remaining Colonial market houses. The museum includes local artifacts and artwork, and a special exhibit focuses on Fredericksburg's role in the Civil War (540-371-3037).

On leaving the museum turn left, and **St. George's Church (5)** will be on your left. The Episcopal parish was founded in 1732; this church building was constructed in 1849. Step inside and see the stained-glass windows, one of which is a memorial to Mary Washington, the mother of our first president. Three windows were made by Louis Comfort Tiffany (540-373-4133).

Opposite the church you'll see the **National Bank Museum (6)** at 900 Princess Anne Street. A Federal-style building dating from 1820, this was originally the Farmer's Bank. Now restored, the museum documents and exhibits banking materials, including a scale for weighing gold dust. Letter, certificates, and bank notes (both genuine and counterfeit) are on display (540-899-3243).

Continue along Princess Anne Street and cross George Street. The **court house (7)** will be on the left at number 815. The first courthouse was built on this site in 1739. The Gothic Revival building you now see was designed by James Renwick in 1852. Renwick also designed New York's St. Patrick's Cathedral and the Smithsonian Castle.

Beyond the courthouse, at number 803, is the **George Washington Masonic Museum (8),** which displays a fine collection of Masonic memorabilia and artwork. A highlight of the collection is an original Gilbert Stuart portrait of George Washington (540-373-5885).

Retrace your steps on Princess Anne Street to George Street. Turn left and the **Presbyterian Church (9)** will be on the left. Clara Barton nursed wounded Civil War soldiers here, and the scars left by cannonballs may be seen on the church walls.

Turn right onto Charles Street. The Masonic Cemetery (1784) will be on the left. It is next to the **James Monroe Museum and Library (10)** at 908 Charles

Street. Monroe was the fifth president of the United States, from 1817 to 1825. This was his law office from 1786 to 1789. The office is furnished with Louis XVI pieces Monroe purchased while he was the U.S. minister to Paris. The museum and library have the largest collection of James Monroe's books, papers, and other memorabilia. A visit includes a video presentation, and visitors are welcome to tour the museum's walled garden (540-654-1053).

Continue on Charles Street and cross William Street, where a sidewalk marker is a grim reminder that this was the site of the town's **slave auction block (11).**

Walk two more blocks on Charles Street and **Mary Washington's House (12)** will be on the left at number 1200. George Washington bought this house for his mother in 1772, and she lived here until she died in 1789. Open to the public, the house displays many of Mrs. Washington's cherished possessions. Be sure to visit the garden, which has her sundial and some of the very boxwood she planted (540-373-1569).

On leaving Mary Washington's House turn left onto Charles Street and then left again onto Fauquier Street. Walk three blocks to Washington Avenue and make another left. Kenmore will be on the left. Before entering, note the two monuments across the way on islands in the middle of Washington Avenue. The stone on the left is dedicated to explorer George Rogers Clark, who lived in Fredericksburg before his 1803 expedition with Meriwether Lewis. On the right is a statue of Hugh Mercer, modeled by Richmond sculptor Edward Valentine in 1906. Now visit **Kenmore Plantation and Gardens (13).** Having seen houses belonging to George Washington's mother and brother, you will now see his sister

Betty's home. Betty and her husband, Col. Fielding Lewis, built this Tidewater Georgian manor house about 1770. The large, elegant home is beautifully decorated with 18th-century furnishings. Kenmore's best-known feature is undoubtedly the outstanding decorative plasterwork that embellishes the ceilings. In addition to the manor house you may visit the gardens and the Crowingshield Museum, which has a diorama of Fredericksburg and a permanent exhibit of local furniture, silver, portraits, and other artifacts. The Marquis de Lafayette was a guest at Kenmore, and today visitors are served tea and gingerbread, just as he was (540-373-3381, www.kenmore.org).

Option A: To view Mary Washington's grave, monument, and meditation rock turn right onto Washington Avenue and look for the obelisk on the opposite side of the street. It marks Mrs. Washington's favored spot for quiet time and solitude. She died in 1789 and was buried here. The present monument was completed and dedicated by President Grover Cleveland in 1894. In the grassy island in front of the grave is the Thomas Jefferson Religious Freedom Monument. Dedicated in 1932, it commemorates Jefferson's initiative, the Virginia Statute for Religious Freedom, which began with a meeting in Fredericksburg in 1777. The statute was a model for the First Amendment to the Bill of Rights.

On leaving Kenmore turn left onto Washington Avenue and walk two blocks to William Street. Note the **cemetery gates (14)** on the right. The gates lead to two burial grounds: the City Cemetery (1844) on the left and the Confederate Cemetery (1867) on the right. The bronze statue of the soldier was dedicated "To the Confederate Dead" in 1884. Federal soldiers killed in local battles are buried in Fredericksburg National Cemetery.

Option B: Fredericksburg National Cemetery is almost a mile from here. To visit the cemetery, turn right onto William Street and left onto Sunken Road. The cemetery will be on the right just before Lafayette Boulevard. The Fredericksburg Battlefield Visitor Center is at that intersection (to the left) at 1013 Lafayette Boulevard (540-371-0802).

Resuming the walk at Washington Avenue and William Street, turn left (east) onto William Street, walking toward the historic district and the river. Turn right onto Prince Edward Street and then left onto Hanover Street. When you reach Caroline Street the visitors center will be on the right and you will have completed the loop.

Also Nearby

Fredericksburg and Spotsylvania County National Military Park and Chatham, an 18th-century estate and Civil War hospital where Clara Barton and Walt Whitman nursed (540-371-0802, 540-786-2880, www.nps.gov/frsp/)

George Washington's Ferry Farm (540-370-0732, www.kenmore.org)

Belmont, artist Gari Melcher's estate (540-654-1015, www.simplyfredericksburg.com/history/belmont.shtml)

12 · Richmond

Directions: *By car:* From the Capital Beltway take I-95 south to exit 74C (Broad Street). Follow Broad Street (US 60) west. Turn left onto Ninth Street and enter Capitol Square. *By public transportation:* Amtrak (1-800-USA-RAIL, www.amtrak.com) and Greyhound (1-800-231-2222, www.greyhound.com) serve Richmond.

In 1607 John Smith and Christopher Newport sailed up the James River, exploring this area. Fort Charles was built on this site in 1644 and in 1733 the growing settlement was named after the English town Richmond upon Thames. Richmond replaced Williamsburg as Virginia's capital in 1779. In 1861 the city became the capital of the Confederacy. On April 3, 1865, Gen. Ulysses S. Grant entered Richmond. Citizens evacuated in haste, torching the tobacco warehouses as they left. Much of the city's business district was also destroyed by fire. During Reconstruction, Richmond rallied, and its economy rebounded.

Begin the tour at Capitol Square. The neoclassical **State Capitol (1)** was begun in 1785 according to plans drawn by Thomas Jefferson. Jefferson's model was La Maison Carrée, a first-century Roman temple in Nîmes, France. Completed in 1792, it was the first mod-

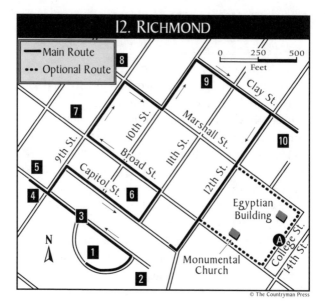

ern full-scale replica of a classical Roman temple. At first the central portion of the capitol you see today stood alone for over a century; the wings were added in 1906. Step inside. In the rotunda is a life-size marble statue of George Washington sculpted by the French artist Jean-Antoine Houdon. Those who knew the president and saw the statue agreed that Houdon had created a perfect likeness. The Marquis de Lafayette remarked, "That is the man himself. I can almost realize he is going to move." Washington is surrounded by marble busts of seven other presidents, all of them born in Virginia: Jefferson, Madison, Monroe, Harrison, Tyler, Taylor, and Wilson. Be sure to visit the museum in the adjoining chamber (804-698-1788).

On leaving the capitol walk down the path to the

Governor's Mansion (2). The house was designed by the famed Boston architect Alexander Parris and completed in 1812. It is said to be the nation's oldest continuously occupied governor's mansion. The house was spared during Richmond's evacuation in 1865 and survived a fire ignited by a Christmas tree in 1926. The mansion has undergone a multimillion-dollar renovation and is open to the public for tours (804-371-2642).

There are two additional points to see before leaving the capitol grounds. The equestrian **statue of George Washington (3)** is surrounded by statues of other Virginia heroes and notables, and was dedicated in 1858. The base of the monument was designed by Robert Mills, who also designed the Washington Monument in the nation's capital. The statues were modeled by Thomas Crawford. Note also the bell tower. Built in 1824, it serves as a visitors center today.

Exit the capitol grounds at Grace and Ninth Streets. **St. Paul's Episcopal Church (4)** will be just ahead on the left. This Greek Revival building was completed in 1845. Pass through the Corinthian columns on the portico, enter the church, and admire its Tiffany windows and superb decorative plaster motifs on the ceiling. Jefferson Davis, president of the Confederacy, was attending Palm Sunday services at St. Paul's on April 2, 1865, when he was told that Grant was advancing and about to take Richmond.

The classical revival **St. Peter's Roman Catholic Church (5)** is just across East Grace Street. It was built in 1835 and for many years was used as a cathedral.

Walk along Ninth Street and turn right onto Broad Street. The **Old City Hall (6)** is at 1001 East Broad. Completed in 1894, it is a Victorian High Gothic design of Elijah E. Meyers. The exterior is Richmond granite. The interior atrium is a blaze of color, its columns, pointed arches, and wall spaces either gilded or painted in vivid tones of blue and red.

Reverse direction and walk one block to the corner of Broad and Ninth Streets. The **Library of Virginia (7)** will be in front of you on the right at 800 East Broad. Founded in 1823, the library's collection of books and records has grown, and it has had several Richmond locations, arriving at its present location in 1997. The library has permanent and changing exhibits on Virginia history, a book shop, and a cafe (804-692-3736, www.lva.lib.va.us).

Return to Ninth Street and walk to the corner of Marshall Street. The **Home of John Marshall (8)** is on the left at 818 East Marshall Street. Marshall was Chief Justice of the U.S. Supreme Court from 1801 to 1835. His house, built in 1790, contains many original furnishings and artifacts and is open to the public (804-648-7998).

Walk on Marshall Street from Ninth to Tenth Street. Turn left onto 10th Street and right onto Clay Street. The **Richmond History Center (9)** will be on the right at 1015 East Clay Street. The center has been collecting objects relating to Richmond history and preserving and presenting them since 1894. It includes a general collection of one million objects from Virginia. The fine arts collection has paintings, sculptures, and other works of and by Virginians from the 18th century to the present. The decorative arts collection has over 25,000 objects, including an extensive collection of furniture manufactured in Richmond. The industrial artifact collection documents the city's businesses, including its significant tobacco trade. In addition to the museum and its collections, visitors may tour the restored and furnished Wickham House. An 1812 Alexander Parris design, every room is open to visitors so that they may see life in this house as lived by the family and their slaves. Finally, the center has a truly remarkable treasure: the intact studio of Edward V. Valentine. Born in Richmond in 1838, Valentine studied sculpture in Europe. Among his most famous works: the Recumbent Lee at the general's burial chapel on the campus of Washington and Lee University, in Lexington, Virginia. The center also has a shop and restaurant (804-649-0711, www.valentinemuseum.com/).

Resume your walk on Clay Street. Just beyond 12th Street the **Museum and White House of the Confederacy (10)** will be on the right. Jefferson Davis, President of the Confederate States of America, lived in this house with his family from 1861 to 1865. The Museum of the Confederacy has the world's most complete and comprehensive collection of Confederate artifacts: flags, paintings, uniforms, weapons, models, photographs, and other memorabilia. The Haversack Store, selling items relating to the Confederacy, is also a part of the museum complex (804-649-1861, www.moc.org).

Return to Capitol Square and the starting point of this tour by way of 12th Street.

Option A: Two architecturally significant buildings are on a short detour. From 12th Street turn left onto Marshall Street and walk to the corner of College Street. Note the Egyptian Building. The architectural revivals of the early19th century took many forms: Greek, classical, Gothic, and others. This is one of the finest examples of the Egyptian Revival style in America. Designed by

Dining room in the White House of the Confederacy

MUSEUM AND WHITE HOUSE OF THE CONFEDERACY, RICHMOND, VA

Thomas Stewart, it was built in 1845 and has always been a medical school. Be sure to stop and take a look at the mummies on the cast-iron fence.

Walk along College Street and turn right onto Broad Street. Monumental Church will be on the right. On December 26, 1811, tragedy struck the city when Richmond Theater burned, claiming the lives of 72 citizens, including the governor. This neoclassical church, a Robert Mills work, was built over a common grave for the fire victims. Completed in 1814, it was an Episcopal church until 1965. Today this National Historic Landmark is owned by the Historic Richmond Foundation.

Also Nearby

Agecroft Hall (804-353-4241)
Edgar Allan Poe Museum (804-648-5523)
Hollywood Cemetery (804-648-8501)
Maggie L. Walker National Historic Site (804-771-2017)
Maymont (804-358-7166)
St. John's Episcopal Church (804-643-5589)
Science Museum of Virginia (804-659-1727)
Virginia House (804-353-4251)
Virginia Museum of Fine Arts (804-340-1400)
Wilton (804-282-5936)

13 • Williamsburg: The Best of the Colonial City

Directions: *By car:* From the Capital Beltway take I-95 south to Richmond, then I-295 south to I-64 east to Williamsburg. Take exit 238 and follow signs to the visitors center. *By public transportation:* Both Amtrak (1-800-USA-RAIL, www.amtrak.com) and Greyhound (1-800-231-2222, www.greyhound.com) serve Williamsburg.

Mention Williamsburg to most people and their mind's eye envisions gracious 18th-century houses, well-manicured English boxwood gardens, tavern rooms warmed by roaring fires, coaches pulled by handsome horses, and byways traversed by men sporting britches and tricorner hats and ladies dressed in the ample skirts so popular in the 1700s. And this is an accurate perception of Williamsburg today.

Set between the York and James Rivers, Middle Plantation (as it was first named) was settled in 1733. Sixty years later the College of William and Mary was opened, the second college America (Harvard had been founded in 1636). When Jamestown burned for a third time in 1698, the colony's capital was moved to Williamsburg—renamed in honor of Britain's King

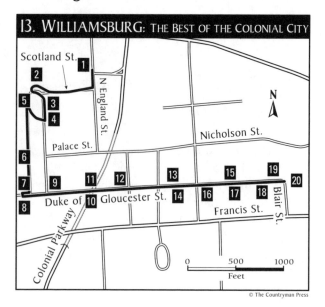

13. WILLIAMSBURG: THE BEST OF THE COLONIAL CITY

© The Countryman Press

William III. Williamsburg grew and flourished in the 18th century. When the state capital was moved to Richmond in 1780, Williamsburg became a quieter town and a shadow of its former self. Fortunately, however, many of its colonial buildings survived.

The restoration of Williamsburg to its colonial splendor was the work and inspiration of the Reverend W.A.R. Goodwin. An Episcopal priest, Goodwin was called to Williamsburg's Bruton Parish Church in 1903 and restored it to its colonial appearance. But his vision of 18th-century restoration extended far beyond the churchyard. In 1926 he shared his dream with John D. Rockefeller Jr. The two men toured Williamsburg, and Rockefeller agreed to finance the restoration of the entire town. It was a mammoth project project covering 3,000 acres. More than 80 colonial building were restored, 700 modern buildings were removed, and more than 400 colonial buildings rebuilt on their original sites. The project is ongoing as excavations continue.

This book includes two self-guided walking tours of Colonial Williamsburg. The first concentrates on Duke of Gloucester Street (the town's main street) and its most popular sites. The second tour leads down Williamsburg's quieter, less-traveled paths. The vast majority of the houses, public buildings, shops, museums, and restaurants featured on both walks are owned and operated by the Colonial Williamsburg Foundation (757-220-7645, 1-800-447-8679, www.colonialwilliamsburg.org).

Begin at the visitors center, where there is parking, an orientation film, information, a restaurant, and a shop. You may walk Williamsburg's streets free of charge, but tickets are needed for admission to most historic sites; they are sold here and at several other sites throughout the historic area.

From the visitors center follow the footpath to the historic area. The **Gateway Building (1)** will be at the end of the path; tickets are sold here. Facing the Gateway Building turn left and then make an immediate right to the **Governor's Palace (2).** Construction of the palace began in 1706. Governor Alexander Spotswood arrived in 1710, and it was under his direction that the palace was embellished with some of the finest furnishings in the colonies. Formal gardens were also added. Completed in 1722, an addition was built in 1752. The last Royal Governor fled Williamsburg in 1775. Thomas Jefferson and Patrick Henry lived in the palace when they were governors. In 1781, a year after the capital was moved to Richmond, the palace was converted for use as a military hospital, and soldiers wounded in Yorktown were treated here. That same year the palace burned to the ground. When Williamsburg was restored in the 1920s, the town's high school stood on this site. The school was removed and excavations revealed the palace's original foundation walls and floors. Rebuilt in the 1930s and furnished with period pieces, the palace is every bit as impressive as it was in the 18th century. Tour the house and the gardens (ticket required). An interesting aside: President Ronald Reagan used the palace to entertain seven heads of state during the international Summit of Industrialized Nations in 1983.

When you leave the palace and face the Palace Green, the **Thomas Everard House (3)** will be on the left. This clapboard house was built in 1718 and bought by Everard in 1755. He lived here for the next 25 years. An orphan, Everard became a wealthy businessman, the clerk of York County Court, and Williamsburg's mayor. An exhibit tells more about the lives of his family and his slaves.

Just step away you'll see the **Play Booth Theater (4),** reconstructed on the site of an early 18th-century theater. Performances of the period are presented here by professional actors.

The **Robert Carter House (5)** is on the opposite side of the Palace Green. Built in 1746, the house was owned by successive generations of the Carter family, one of Virginia's wealthiest. Interestingly, the Carter House was also a governor's residence in the 1750s while the palace was undergoing renovations.

Walk along Palace Street a few steps. The **Wythe**

House (6) will be on the right. The redbrick house was designed by Col. Richard Taliaferro. His daughter married George Wythe, and they lived here from 1755 to 1791. George Washington lived in this house during the siege of Yorktown in 1781. French General Rochambeau later lived here, too.

Walk to the next corner and **Bruton Parish Church (7)** will be on your right. The Episcopal parish was named after an English church on the River Brue in Somerset, where many of the parishioners had immigrated from. Founded in 1674 by joining parishes dating to the 1630s, Bruton's first rector was the Reverend Rowland Jones. His great-granddaughter was Martha Washington. Alexander Spotswood, the governor-architect who directed the building of the Governor's Palace, designed this church in 1711. Forty years later the church was enlarged. The bell tower was added in 1769; it houses a bell from the same period. Note the bust of the Reverend W.A.R. Goodwin at the base of the tower. Goodwin restored this church to its Colonial design.

Step inside the church. The high box pews provided privacy and protection from drafts in the unheated building. Some of the pews have been labeled with the names of patriots and presidents who have worshiped here, including George Washington. Over the high altar note the tablets inscribed with the Apostles' Creed, the Lord's Prayer, and the Ten Commandments. In Virginia Anglicanism was the official religion, church attendance was required for officials, and these tablets were required to be displayed over the altar. Above the altar's reredos and tablets is an organ dating to 1785. The thronelike chair on the left was the governor's pew. The bronze lectern next to it was a gift of President

ROBERT J. REGALBUTO

The Capitol

Theodore Roosevelt at the time of the Jamestown Ter-
centennial in 1907. The baptismal font originally stood
in the church at Jamestown. George Washington stood
as godfather at this font on fourteen occasions.

When you leave the churchyard you will be on the
Duke of Gloucester Street—Williamburg's main street.
Just across the way is the **Harnessmaker-Saddler (Tal-
iaferro-Cole) Shop (8).** This is one of the many businesses that line this thoroughfare.

Walk east on the Duke of Gloucester Street. On the
left, just beyond the Palace Green, will be the **James
Geddy House and the Geddy Foundry (9).** Geddy
was a gunsmith. He and his sons manufactured not
only firearms but also bullets and various tools. The
Shoemaker's Shop just across the Duke of Gloucester
Street may also be visited. As in so many of Williamsburg's shops, craftsmen may be observed at work today
making the same products their predecessors did more
than two centuries ago.

Just a few steps away will be the **Magazine (10).** A

storage facility for arms and munitions, the Magazine is another Governor Spotswood design. Built in 1715, the building has a fascinating history. After the Revolution it was used as a Baptist church. During the Civil War it was returned to its original use as an arsenal by the Confederate army. Following the Civil War the Magazine was used as a dancing school, a livery stable, and as a museum of local memorabilia. The Association for the Preservation of Virginia Antiquities (APVA) restored the building in the 1930s. The colonial firearms and equipment in the Magazine and Guardhouse are used in presentations given by costumed interpreters.

The **Courthouse (11),** built in 1771, is opposite the Magazine. Its stone steps were imported from London. The four Ionic stone columns that were meant to support the portico, however, never did make the journey from England to America. Note the stocks and pillory outside the Courthouse where many of today's visitors pause for picture-taking.

Next is **Chowning's Tavern (12).** Opened by Josiah Chowing in 1766, the tavern serves hearty meals in a Colonial atmosphere to this day.

As you continue your stroll east on the Duke of Gloucester Street, the **Printer, Bookbinding, and Post Office (13)** will be on the left. The shop is well stocked with reproductions of 18th-century English and colonial prints. and also carries a full line of Colonial Williamsburg Foundation's publications.

A few steps away, across the street is the **Mary Stith House (14).** Mary Stith was the daughter of William Stith, one-time president of the College of William and Mary. When she died in 1813 she bequeathed this house, property, and a portion of her estate to her "coloured people." Reconstructed, the house has presentations by actors portraying 18th-century Williamsburg personages. At the James Anderson Blacksmith Shop in back of the Stith house blacksmiths work with 18th-century tools and equipment.

After crossing Botetourt Street you are on the final block of commercial activity before reaching the capitol. On the right will be the wigmaker and on the left you will see the milliner, silversmith, the Pasteur and Galt Apothecary Shop, and the **Raleigh Tavern (15).** Both the Raleigh Tavern and **Wetherburn's Tavern (16),** across the street, are now museums. The taverns clustered near the capitol provided food, refreshment, and lodging to government officials. Continuing in this tradition, the **King's Arms Tavern (17)** and **Shield's Tavern (18),** both on the right as you face the capitol, are operating restaurants feeding today's hungry travelers. Baked goods are sold at Raleigh Tavern.

As you approach the capitol the redbrick **Secretary's Office (19)** will be on the left. Built in 1748 as a storage facility for public records, the office now houses a small museum that focuses on the American Revolution, and a shop where tickets, books, and souvenirs are sold.

As the reader will no doubt agree, the Duke of Gloucester Street is a long, dramatic approach to the **Capitol (20).** Williamsburg became Virginia's capital in 1699 after the previous capital, Jamestown, burned for the third time. Williamsburg's first capitol was built on this site from 1701 to 1705. It burned in 1747 and was replaced by a second in 1753. When the state capital moved to Richmond in 1780, Williamsburg's capitol was used successively as a hospital, a school, and finally a courthouse until it burned to the ground in 1832.

The property passed through the hands of the APVA to the Colonial Williamsburg Foundation. Excavations in the late 1920s uncovered the foundation of the first capitol on this site, which is reconstructed here. Its H-shaped floor plan reflects the building's use by a bicameral legislature (the House of Burgesses and the Council); both chambers are connected by a passageway.

The Capitol is the culmination of this walk and is open to visitors. Should you wish to return to the visitors center, an alternative to walking is a shuttle service provided by the Colonial Williamsburg Foundation.

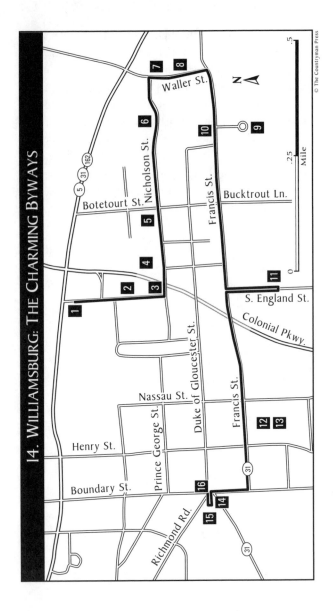

14. WILLIAMSBURG: THE CHARMING BYWAYS

© The Countryman Press

Waller St.

Botetourt St.

Nicholson St.

Francis St.

Bucktrout Ln.

S. England St.

Colonial Pkwy.

Nassau St.

Prince George St.

Duke of Gloucester St.

Francis St.

Henry St.

Boundary St.

Richmond Rd.

N

0   .25   .5
Mile

14 • Williamsburg:
The Charming Byways

Directions: *By car:* From the Capital Beltway take I-95 south to Richmond, then I-295 south to I-64 east to Williamsburg. Take exit 238 and follow the signs to the visitors center. *By public transportation:* Both Amtrak (1-800-USA-RAIL, www.amtrak.com) and Greyhound (1-800-231-2222, www.greyhound.com) serve Williamsburg.

This tour will lead you along Williamsburg's less-visited lanes. These roads and paths are quieter, but no less picturesque, than the city's more popular thoroughfares.

The vast majority of the houses, public buildings, shops, museums, and restaurants on the tour are owned and operated by the Colonial Williamsburg Foundation (757-220-7645, 1-800-447-8679, www.colonialwilliamsburg.org). For more on this organization and its origins, see tour 13, "Williamsburg: The Best of the Colonial City."

Begin at the visitors center, where there is parking, an orientation film, information, a restaurant, and a shop. You may walk Williamsburg's streets free of charge, but tickets are needed for admission to most historic sites;

they are sold here and at several other sites throughout the historic area. Start your walk at the visitors center and follow the footpath to the historic area. Once there, if you have not already done so at the visitors center, you may purchase tickets at the **Gateway Building (1).**

Facing the front door of the Gateway Building, turn left onto North England Street. Stop at **Robertson's Windmill (2).** In colonial times townsfolk would bring their grain here to be ground, making flour they used to bake their bread. The cooper's work (making wooden buckets and the like) and other rural trades are demonstrated next to the windmill. Walk just a few steps farther down the street and carpenters may be seen at work using 18th-century tools and construction methods.

The **Peyton Randolph House (3)** is the dark red house to the left on the next corner. The oldest part of the house, which faces North England Street, dates to 1718. Peyton Randolph was a lawyer, a leader in the fight for independence, and eventually became president of the Continental Congress meeting in Philadelphia. His cousin, Thomas Jefferson, acquired Randolph's library, which became the foundation for the Library of Congress. Furnished with American and English period pieces, the house is open to visitors, who are afforded a glimpse at the roles played in the American Revolution by Randolph, his family, and his slaves.

North England Street ends at Nicholson Street; turn left. The **Brickmaker's Yard (4)** will be on the left, and beyond that the cabinetmaker. Anthony Hay owned this shop for 10 years, starting in 1756. He then bought the Raleigh Tavern on the Duke of Gloucester Street. Visit the shop and see a cabinetmaker and his assistant creating 18th-century-style furnishings.

Just a few steps away, at the corner of Nicholson and Botetourt Streets, is the **Tenant House (5),** which offers another perspective on life as lived in the colonial city.

Nicholson Street leads to the **Public Gaol (6),** built in 1701. The small redbrick building housed the jail-keeper and his family as well as prisoners. The wall enclosed the prison yard, where inmates exercised. The gaol tour recounts the conditions of 18th-century prison life. Shackles and other artifacts unearthed from this site are on display.

At the end of Nicholson Street turn right onto Waller Street. The **Benjamin Powell House (7)** will be on the left. Powell was a builder whose works may be still seen: Bruton Church's tower and belfry, and the Public Hospital (seen later on this walk). His house is open seasonally.

Continue to walk along Waller Street and **Christina Campbell's Tavern (8)** will be on the left. Still an operating restaurant, the tavern was a favorite dining spot for George Washington.

At the end of Waller Street turn right onto Francis Street and then make an immediate left on the drive approaching **Bassett Hall (9),** the Williamsburg home of John D. Rockefeller Jr. and his wife, Abby Aldrich Rockefeller. After Rockefeller agreed to finance Williamsburg's restoration, he purchased this house and nearly 600 acres surrounding it. The house is named for Burwell Bassett, who owned the property from 1800 to 1839. He was a nephew of Martha Washington. The gardens and the house, comfortably furnished as it was when the financier lived here, are open for tours.

On leaving Bassett Hall return to Francis Street.

Opposite the driveway on your left is the **Gunsmith (Ayscough House) (10).** A visit includes demonstrations of the manufacture of firearms, muskets, locks, and other products made from iron, brass, wood, and steel.

Walk west on Francis Street, pass the Williamsburg Inn, and turn left onto South England Street. The **Abby Aldrich Rockefeller Folk Art Museum (11)** will be on the left. Mrs. Rockefeller was a pioneer in recognizing and appreciating the beauty and value of early American folk art. She began her collection in the 1920s and in 1939 gave it to the Colonial Williamsburg Foundation. A collection of 400 works at that time, it has grown to include more than 2,500 objects. John D. Rockefeller Jr. built the museum as a memorial to his wife in 1957, and the facility was enlarged in 1991. There are permanent and changing exhibits, a museum store, and a research library.

Return to Francis Street, turn left, and stop at the **Public Hospital (12).** The first institution of its kind in North America, the hospital was opened in 1773 to care for the mentally ill. It burned to the ground in 1885. Now reconstructed, the hospital is the entryway and access to the adjacent **DeWitt Wallace Decorative Arts Museum (13).** Built in 1985 with funds bequeathed by Reader's Digest founder DeWitt Wallace, the museum provides ample space to exhibit Colonial Williamsburg Foundation's extensive collection of 17th- and 18th-century English and American decorative arts. Furniture, paintings, prints, silver, brass, and ceramics are on permanent display as is a collection of costumes. The museum's walled garden is a memorial to Wallace's wife and *Reader's Digest* cofounder, Lila Acheson Wallace.

Visitors watch the reconstruction of an outbuilding at the Peyton Randolph House.

Exit through the Public Hospital and return to Francis Street. Turn left and walk to the end of the street. Then turn right onto South Boundary Street. Mind the traffic and cross the road to the **College of William and Mary (14),** on the left. When it was founded in 1693 the only other college in the American colonies was Harvard, which had been founded in 1636. Named for England's reigning couple, the school received its charter from King William III and his consort, Queen Mary. Approach the **Wren Building (15).** If not designed by the London architect Sir Christopher Wren, this building was certainly heavily influenced by his work. The construction began in 1695, and its chapel was added in 1732. Over the span of three centuries the building has endured three fires, two wars, and structural alterations and improvements. In 1928 the Wren Building was the first in Williamsburg restored through the generosity of John D. Rockefeller Jr. Visit the interior and see the great hall, chapel, and class-room.

When you leave the Wren Building and return to town you will be flanked by twin collegiate buildings: the President's House on the left and the Brafferton on the right.

Continue to walk straight ahead on the Duke of Gloucester Street to **Merchant's Square (16).** A cluster of shops and restaurants, Merchant's Square is the endpoint of this tour. To return to the visitors center walk down the Duke of Gloucester Street, turn left onto Palace Street, and the path to the center will be to the right of the Governor's Palace. If you've walked far enough, there is a shuttle bus from the corner of Duke of Gloucester and Henry Streets.

Also Nearby

Carter's Grove Plantation (757-220-7645, 1-800-447-8679)

15 · Jamestown

Directions: *By car:* Take I-95 south to Richmond, then take I-295 south to I-64 east. Take exit 242, the Colonial Parkway, to Jamestown. *By public transportation:* From Williamsburg, Williamsburg Transit (757-259-4111) has a seasonal shuttle service to Jamestown. Alternately, it is a short cab ride.

James Cittie, named in honor of King James I, was the scene of many firsts. It was the first permanent British settlement on this continent (1607), it set up the first form of representative government in America (1619), it had the first tobacco plantation in the colonies, and it was the site of the first Anglican (Episcopal) church in North America (1607). A more somber Jamestown first was the introduction of slavery to America, sometime before 1630.

Unlike other colonies, James Cittie was not founded as a haven for religious or political refugees. An enterprise of the Virginia Company of London, its purpose was purely economic. The enterprise was not a success. Disease and starvation claimed the lives of 6,000 of the 7,300 colonist by 1627. There were Indian attacks in 1622 and 1644, and the town was thrice destroyed by fire (in 1600, 1676, and 1698). Following the last fire Virginia's capital was moved from Jamestown to

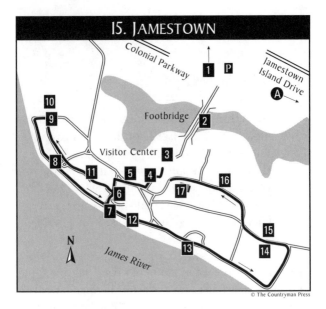

Williamsburg. Jamestown was left abandoned, but not forgotten. Celebrations in 1807, 1857, 1907, and one in 1957, which was attended by Queen Elizabeth II, commemorated the colony's founding and its significance. Another celebration is planned for 2007 when Jamestown will be 400 years old. Monuments dedicated during the jubilees are noted on this walking tour.

There are two sites to visit in Jamestown. Jamestown Settlement recreates the colonial fort and Powhatan Indian village, and three tall ships are docked in the James River, all staffed by guides in period costume (757-253-5112, 1-888-593-4682, www.historyisfun. org). Jamestown Settlement is near the Original Site, also known as Historic Jamestowne, a National Historical Park on the very spot where the colony stood. This walking tour will explore the Original Site—Historic Jamestowne—which is open to the public by the Association for the Preservation of Virginia Antiquities (APVA) (804-648-1889, www.apva.org) in partnership with the National Park Service (757-229-1733, www.nps.gov/colo).

As you approach Historic Jamestowne your first stop should be the **glasshouse (1),** on the right. Glassblowing was one of the settlement's earliest industries, introduced by Polish and German craftsmen in 1608 who were joined by Venetian glassblowers in the 1620s. Today visitors may see artisans create bottles and other glassware, which are for sale.

From the parking lot cross the Pitch and Tar Swamp on the **footbridge (2).** Pitch and tar were extracted from the pine trees along the banks of the swamp to be used as caulking for ships.

The **Visitor Center (3)** will be on the right. Its galleries include artifacts excavated from the site, and there are continuous screenings of an excellent orientation film. The center also houses the Museum Book Store.

When you leave the visitors center you will see a 103-foot-high **obelisk (4).** Built in 1907, this New Hampshire–granite monument was dedicated at the 300th anniversary of the settlement's founding.

Continue down the path past the obelisk and turn right onto The Great Road. On the right will be a **statue of Pocahontas (5).** The daughter of tribal chief Powhatan, Pocahontas is probably best known for saving the life of Capt. John Smith. According to Smith's account, he had his head on the block to be decapitated at the hands of her Indian captors, when 13-year-old Pocahontas intervened, begging her father to spare

Smith, which he did. Pocahontas was baptized Lady Rebecca and married the Englishman John Rolfe. In 1616 the couple made a voyage to England, where they were presented at court. Pocahontas became the darling of London society. On the eve of what was to be her return trip to America, Lady Rebecca contracted small-pox and died in England at the age of 22. She is buried at Gravesend, in Kent. This monument, modeled by William Ordway Partridge, was dedicated in 1922.

Walk along The Great Road just a few more steps. Turn left, and **Jamestown Church (6)** will be on the left. This, the first Anglican (Episcopal) parish in America, was founded under the auspices of the Bishop of London in 1607. The massive redbrick tower is all that remains of the church which was built here in 1639. Once 46 feet high, the tower is 18 feet square; its walls are 3 feet thick. Pass through the portal and enter the Memorial Church, a reconstruction dedicated during the Tercentenary in 1907. This is the fifth Anglican church built in Jamestown. The parishoners worshiped in a tent (1607), frame buildings (1608 and again in 1617), and brick buildings (in 1639 and this one in 1907). In 1614 Pocahontas and John Rolfe were married in the frame church, and on July 30, 1619, the church was the meeting place for the first representative legislative assembly in North America. A gift of the National Society of Colonial Dames of America, the church is maintained today by the APVA.

With your back to the church tower turn left and walk toward the James River. The imposing **statue of Capt. John Smith (7),** who lived from 1580 to 1631, was modeled by William Couper and dedicated in 1909. Smith sailed from England, disembarking at the

ROBERT J. REGALBUTO

Old Church Tower

site of the future Jamestown on May 14, 1607. He became Jamestown's governor, traded with the Indians, explored and mapped Virginia's waterways, and directed the construction of the early settlement. Injured in 1609, he returned to England for a time, crossing the Atlantic again in 1614, this time exploring and mapping the region he named New England. Smith ultimately returned to England and died there in 1631.

Facing the James turn right and walk on the path parallel to the riverbank. Your next stop is the **Dale House**

Archaeology Laboratory (8). In addition to archaeological exhibits the laboratory has an interactive video. More than a museum, the laboratory is a work space for conservators whom you may observe at work. The Carrot Tree Cafe is next door.

Walk to the end of the path and turn right. **The Memorial Cross (9)** was dedicated by Queen Elizabeth II during the jubilee in 1957 and marks the spot where 300 settlers were buried during the starving time (the winter of 1609–10).

Next to the Memorial Cross are the **foundations (10)** of the third and fourth statehouses, both built and replaced in the 17th century.

Walk the length of the path that starts at the Memorial Cross. You will pass the laboratory on the right and, farther on, the **Reverend Robert Hunt Shrine (11)** on the left, dedicated to the settlement's first Anglican priest. At the end of the path turn right, return to the river, and then turn left.

Stop at the **1607 James Fort Archaeological Site (12).** The Association for the Preservation of Virginia Antiquities (APVA) discovered this site in 1996 and has since conducted excavations. It is estimated that 85 percent of the fort remains here. To date over 400,000 artifacts have been discovered on this site. Excavations are ongoing, and visitors may witness the unearthing of even more.

Continue to walk parallel to the river. The **Original Port (13)** will be on the right and the remains of an 18th-century farm are on the left. Next you'll see the site of the house built in 1618 for gunsmith John Jackson. Follow the path to the left and turn left at the **T** in the path. This will bring you to the site of the **New Towne**

(14), which was built outside the original fortifications after 1620.

On the right are the **ruins of two houses (15)** built on the same site: the Secretary Kemp House (1639) and the Plantation House of Richard Ambler (1753).

At the next crossing turn right. The **Longhouse (16)** once stood on your right. Built in the 1660s, it was a row of four buildings that included the jail and the town office. Behind the Longhouse stood the work-places of the many tradesmen who helped make the colony self-sufficient: tanners, potters, brewers, an apothecary, and others.

The **Swan Tavern (17)** stood a few feet farther down the road on the left. The 17th-century tavern was at once a private home and an ordinary (or restaurant and inn) frequented by Burgesses and others in town attending meetings of the Virginia Assembly.

Follow the path to The Great Road and you have come full circle.

Option A: The parking lot is the starting point for two loop drives. One is 3 miles long, the other 5 miles. Both are dotted with wayside signs which interpret the agricultural and industrial lives of Jamestown's settlers.

Also Nearby

Jamestown Settlement (757-253-4838, 1-888-593-4682, www.historyisfun.org)

16 · Yorktown

Directions: *By car:* From the Capital Beltway take I-95 south to Richmond. Then take I-295 south to I-64 east. Take exit 242, the Colonial Parkway, to Yorktown. *By public transportation:* Williamsburg transit (757-259-4111) has a seasonal shuttle service between Williamsburg and Yorktown. Alternately, you may take a taxi cab to Yorktown.

Yorktown was the scene of the last major battle of the American Revolution and where British General Charles, Lord Cornwallis, surrendered on October 19, 1781. Within two years the Treaty of Paris was signed.

Though charming, today's Yorktown is a mere shadow of the bustling port and shipping center it was from the 1690s until the Revolution. Twice under siege, first during the Revolution and again under Union forces during the Civil War, Yorktown also suffered and declined from devastating fires in 1814 and 1863.

A town of restored Colonial homes, museums, and shops, Yorktown is a delightful little village to tour on foot. Begin at the visitors center, administered by the National Park Service. Yorktown and Historic Jamestowne, linked by the Colonial Parkway, form the 7,000-acre Colonial National Historical Park (757-898-3400, www.nps.gov/colo). The **Visitor Center (1)** presents

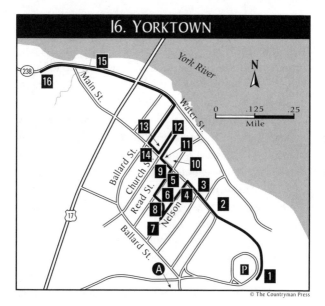

16. YORKTOWN

© The Countryman Press

an orientation film and has a museum, book shop, and other resources. A walkway leads from the visitor center to the **Yorktown Victory Monument (2),** commissioned by the Continental Congress in 1781. Surprisingly a century passed before their wishes were fulfilled with the dedication of this monolith during the 1881 Centennial Celebration. President Chester A. Arthur attended the laying of the cornerstone amid a large gathering and John Philip Sousa led the U.S. Marine Band. The monument combines the work of three men: Richard Morris Hunt, the dean of American architecture; John Q. Adams Ward, the dean of American sculpture; and Henry Van Brunt, architect. Built of white marble, it cost approximately $100,000. A column rises from the four-sided base. The 13 maidens surrounding the column represent the original colonies, and 38 stars rise on the shaft above them, one for each state of the Union in 1881. The Goddess of Liberty crowns the column. Unfortunately, the goddess lost her head to lightning in 1912; a replica replaced the original statue in 1956. A lightning rod was also installed.

From the monument walk to Main Street, turn right, and stop at the **Dudley Digges House (3),** which will be on the right. Though owned by the National Park Service, the house is not open to the public. It was built in 1760 and restored by the NPS two centuries later. Dudley Digges was a member of the House of Burgesses, a Revolutionary War hero, and later rector of Williamsburg's College of William and Mary.

Note the **Sessions House (4)** on Main Street just opposite the Dudley Digges House. Built in 1693, it is believed to be the oldest house standing in town. Just a few steps farther along Main Street, on the left, you will see the **Nelson House (5).** This redbrick mansion dates to 1730. Built for the Scottish merchant Thomas Nelson, it later was inherited by Thomas Nelson Jr. The younger Nelson distinguished himself as a member of the House of Burgesses, a signer of the Declaration of Independence, governor of Virginia, and as a brigadier general, the Commander of the Virginia Militia at the siege of Yorktown in 1781. His house is one of the finest examples of early Georgian architecture extant in the state. Both the mansion and its garden are open to the public by the National Park Service.

Walk down Nelson Street between the Nelson and Sessions houses. The **Smith House (6)** will be on the right. Built by Edmund Smith about 1750, the house was inherited by his daughter Mildred, who married the

Scotsman David Jameson. Jameson was Virginia's lieutenant governor at the time of the siege in 1781.

The **Ballard House (7)** is next. Built in 1720, this frame house was home to the family of merchant sea captain John Ballard. Take the path beyond the Ballard House to the **Poor Potter (8).** The remnants of a large pottery factory dating to the 1720s, this site is opened to visitors by the park service. Excavations at the Poor Potter are ongoing and visitors may observe the progress being made by archaeologists.

Leave the Poor Potter on Read Street and turn right, returning to Main Street. The **Customs House (9),** built in 1721, will be on the left. The port of Yorktown had its own customs collector in colonial times.

The **Pate House (10)** stands opposite the Customs House. Built circa 1700 for the ferryman Thomas Pate, this later became the home of merchant Cole Diggs.

Walk along Main Street and the **Somerwell House (11)** will be on the right. Another dwelling for a York River ferryman, this became a hospital for Union troops during the Civil War. It later became the Yorktown Hotel. More recently restored to its colonial appearance, it is now a private residence.

Walk down Church Street and visit **Grace Church (12).** First known as the York-Hampton Church, the oldest parts of this Anglican house of worship date to 1697. Interestingly, the church was not built with bricks but with marl extracted from the shores of the York River. The church was used as a powder magazine during the Revolution, suffered damage because of it, and was burned during Yorktown's Great Fire in 1814. Standing in ruins for decades, Grace Church was rebuilt in 1848, incorporating parts of the original 17th-

Dudley Digges House with the Victory Monument in the distance

century building. During the Civil War the church became a hospital and its belfry a lookout tower. Visit the churchyard. The earliest grave was dug in 1701. Thomas Nelson Jr. is buried here (757-898-3261).

Return to Main Street and turn right to the **Medical Shop (13).** The office of Dr. Corbin Griffin, a Scottish physician, was built here in the 1760s. Destroyed by fire in 1814, the doctor's office has been rebuilt by the park service and is open to the public.

Across Main Street, to the right, is the **Swan Tavern (14).** The original tavern was built on this site in 1722 and for generations served as a place for lodging, food, and libations. A neighboring building was the old courthouse. Used as a munitions and powder magazine by Union forces during the Civil War, the courthouse exploded in 1863. The tavern was completely destroyed and was rebuilt by the National Park Service in the 1930s. Visitors may visit the tavern's kitchen and stables. Walk down Main Street, pass York Hall on the right, turn right onto Ballard Street, and walk to Water Street at the foot of the hill. Turn left onto Water Street. Walk parallel to the riverfront and pass under the bridge. Stop at the **Waterman's Museum (15).** The museum documents and illustrates the life of the watermen who harvested seafood from Chesapeake Bay from precolonial times to the more recent past. The museum's permanent collection includes boat models, paintings, nautical artifacts, tools, and photographs. Fishing boats have been placed on its grounds. The museum also has a restaurant and a gift shop (757-887-2641, www.visitwilliamsburg.com/watermans_museum.htm).

Facing the York River turn left and walk to the **Yorktown Victory Center (16).** A living history museum sponsored by the Commonwealth of Virginia, the center presents an orientation film, exhibits hundreds of colonial artifacts, and has re-created an 18th-century farm and an army encampment, both of which are staffed by costumed interpreters. The Yorktown Victory Center and Jamestown Settlement are operated by the Jamestown-Yorktown Foundation, and combination tickets to the two sites are available (757-253-4838, 1-888-593-4682, www.historyisfun.org).

This is where your walking tour of Yorktown ends.

Option A: Should you wish to explore the battlefields by car, the National Park Service Visitors Center will provide you with maps of two driving tours. One leads to the Moore House, where British and Continental officers met on October 18, 1781, to negotiate the terms of the surrender.

17 • Norfolk

Directions: *By car:* From the Capital Beltway, take I-95 south to Richmond, then I-295 south to I-64 east to Norfolk, then I-264 west to exit 10. Drive on City Hall Avenue past St. Paul's Boulevard and park at the MacArthur Center. Parking will be validated with admission to the MacArthur Memorial. Alternately, there is free on-street parking on Sundays. *By public transportation:* Greyhound (1-800-231-2222, www.greyhound.com) and Amtrak (1-800-USA-RAIL, www.amtrak.com) have service to Norfolk.

Named for an English county, Norfolk was founded in 1682. In colonial times the town grew as a port and a shipbuilding center. During the American Revolution, as Norfolk alternately was in the hands of British and Continental forces, the town was bombarded by the Tories and later burned by the Patriots. The only remnant of colonial Norfolk is St. Paul's Church, which you will see on this tour. During the 20th century the U.S. Navy's Norfolk facilities grew tremendously. The headquarters for NATO's Supreme Allied Command is located here.

The **General Douglas MacArthur Center (1),** a large shopping mall in the center of downtown Nor-

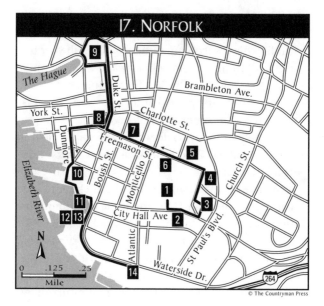

17. NORFOLK

© The Countryman Press

folk, offers parking and is a good starting point for a walking tour of the city. The MacArthur Center's Windows on History displays face City Hall Avenue. Cross City Hall Avenue to the **MacArthur Memorial (2).** General Douglas MacArthur, born in Little Rock, Arkansas, in 1889, graduated from West Point in 1903. As a five-star general, he commanded the Southwest Pacific theater during World War II, oversaw the Allied occupation of Japan following the war, and initially led the United Nations forces in the Korean War. He died in 1964 and chose to be buried in Norfolk, his mother's home city. The MacArthur Memorial is a complex of five buildings. The museum, an 1847 Greek Revival building, was for many years Norfolk's city hall. The general and his wife are interred under the museum's rotunda.

You may also visit nine galleries that recount the general's career and display much of his memorabilia, including his corncob pipe. There is also a theater that screens a 24-minute film, a library and archives, and a gift shop. MacArthur's 1950 Chrysler Imperial limousine is permanently parked at the gift shop (757-441-2965, www.sites.communitylink.org/mac).

Turn right onto City Hall Avenue and walk a block to the Episcopal **St. Paul's Church (3).** General MacArthur's funeral service was held here. The parish, established in 1637, has a long history. The brick church you see today was built in 1739 and is the oldest building standing in Norfolk. In 1776 the British bombarded the city and St. Paul's was the only building to survive. But it was not untouched. You may see a British cannonball permanently lodged in the church's southeast corner. Visit the interior, which has 18th-century decorative elements, such as the tablets behind the high altar, and 19th-century additions, such as the stained-glass windows and the baptismal font. Visit the graveyard. The brick wall that encloses the ¾-acre churchyard was built in 1759. The oldest gravestone is dated 1673. Visit the parish house, which has a museum. Of special note: the museum has the chair in which John Hancock sat when he signed the Declaration of Independence (757-627-4353).

Leave the churchyard at the gate between the church and the parish house museum, at Cumberland Street. Turn right and walk to the **Willoughby Baylor House (4),** at the corner of Freemason Street. Built in 1794, the elegantly furnished house and its 18th-century secret garden are open to the public by the Chrysler Museum of Art (757-333-6283 or 757-441-1526, www.chrysler.org).

Walk along Freemason Street and the **Freemason Baptist Church (5)** will be on the right. An early Gothic Revival design, the church was completed in 1850. Its brick exterior is covered with stucco. The church's first spire, loftier than the present one, was blown down in an 1879 storm. Though the present octagonal spire is newer and shorter, its weathervane is the original and depicts the trumpet blown by the Angel Gabriel. Former presidential candidate Pat Robertson was ordained a minister at this church in 1960.

Just a few steps farther along Freemason Street, the **Moses Myers House (6)** will be on the left. Another Chrysler Museum of Art historic house, this Federal dwelling was built in 1792. It was one of the first brick houses built in Norfolk following the city's destruction during the Revolution, and has been meticulously restored and beautifully furnished. The collection includes portraits of Moses and Eliza Myers painted by Gilbert Stuart. The Garden Club of Virginia continues its ongoing restoration of the property (757-333-6283 or 757-441-1526, www.chrysler.org).

When you leave the Moses Myers House turn left onto Freemason Street. Note the **Epworth Methodist Church (7)** on the right at the corner of Boush Street. This congregation was organized in 1848, and its Romanesque Revival church built in 1894. The chimes in its massive tower may be heard throughout the neighborhood each day at noon.

Continue along Freemason Street just 1 block more to the corner of Duke Street. The **Hunter House Victorian Museum (8)** will be ahead of you on the right. This Richardsonian Romanesque house was built for the Hunter family in 1894. The house is filled with original furnishings, stained-glass windows, and other decorative arts. There is also a collection of Victorian toys (757-623-9814, www.hunterhousemuseum.org/history/family.htm).

Leave Freemason Street and walk up Duke Street the length of 4 short blocks through a stretch of small, nondescript office buildings dotted with an occasional drive-up bank window. This part of this walk may not be the tour's most inspiring, but at the end you will be rewarded with the sight of one of Norfolk's gems: the **Chrysler Museum of Art (9).** The museum is in the trendy Ghent neighborhood—named for the Belgian city in which the treaty that ended the War of 1812 was signed. As you approach the museum look to the right. The handsome post-modern building you see is the Harrison Opera House (757-664-6464, www.sevenavenues.com/harrisonoperahouse).

Walk around the museum to the front door, which is thoughtfully sited at the end of The Hague—an inlet of the Elizabeth River. It is thought the inlet was named for the city of The Hague in the Netherlands, which is known for its world-class art museums. Face the entrance to the Chrysler Museum. Inspired by Italian Renaissance palazzi, construction of the museum began in the 1920s and was completed in 1933. Originally known as the Norfolk Museum of Arts and Sciences, the museum's collection was greatly enhanced in 1971 with a major donation from automobile manufacturing heir Walter P. Chrysler. The museum's building was updated and expanded in 1989. Today its 60 galleries surround a sunlit courtyard and contain an extensive and impressive collection of 30,000 objects representing 5,000 years of art. In addition to paintings by Old Mas-

Battleship Wisconsin

ters and Impressionist and American artists, the museum is widely known for its collection of 7,000 glass pieces, including Tiffany designs and Sandwich glass. A library, shop, and restaurant are also on the premises (757-664-6200, www.chrysler.org).

Retrace your steps down Duke Street to Freemason Street, turn right onto Freemason and then left onto Dunmore Street, passing an impressive series of late 19th-century houses in this, the Freemason Historic District. Dunmore Street ends at the lovely Oriental Garden in which you'll see the **Taiwanese Friendship Pavilion (10).** A gift from the people of Taiwan in 1989, this two-story pagoda is an observation tower overlooking the city and the river. Curiously, the tower's concrete foundation is an old molasses tank.

Continue along the banks of the Elizabeth River. The **U.S.S.** *Wisconsin* **(11)** is docked just ahead. One of the largest battleships ever built for the U.S. Navy, the *Wisconsin*'s statistics are impressive: it is 300 yards long, weighs 45 tons, and had a crew of 3,000 at any given time. She was deployed during World War II, the Korean War, and, most recently, during Operation Desert Storm. Tour the battleship, try its hands-on virtual battlescopes, and participate in the ship design chamber—an interactive theater (1-800-664-1080, www.battleshipwisconsin.com).

The *Wisconsin* is docked alongside **Nauticus: The National Maritime Center (12).** An enormous museum complex, Nauticus includes the Hampton Roads Naval Museum, which documents over 200 years of American naval history, from the Revolution, through the Civil War and the ironclads, to the 20th century to the present. Visit the Aegis Theater, Nauticus Theater, hands-on touch tanks, Shark Touch, interactive exhibits on nautical power and natural power, the National Oceanic and Atmosphere (NOAA) displays, and other changing exhibits. The Nauticus also houses the Banana Pier Gift Shop and a restaurant overlooking the scenic Elizabeth River (1-800-664-1080, www.nauticus.org).

Dwarfed by its massive neighbors Nauticus and the U.S.S. *Wisconsin,* the **Tugboat Museum (13)** proudly holds its own as an historic venue worth exploring. The tug *Huntington* dates to 1933. Now she is retired, and you may visit the engine room below deck, the wheelhouse, captain's quarters, crew's quarters, galley, and saloon. Videos and photographs tell the *Huntington*'s story and explain the role of the small but mighty tugboats (757-627-4884).

Continue parallel to the river along the paths of Town Point Park to **The Waterside (14),** a complex adjacent to the marina that has many eateries and shops (757-627-3300). Your Norfolk historic walking tour ends here. To return to the MacArthur Center walk up Atlantic Street.

Also Nearby

Naval Station Norfolk (757-444-7955)
Norfolk Botanical Garden (757-441-5830)
Hermitage Foundation Museum (757-423-2052)

18 · Portsmouth

Directions: *By car:* From the Capital Beltway take I-95 south to Richmond. Then take I-295 south to I-64 east. Take the I-664 south exit and cross the Monitor-Merrimac Memorial Bridge Tunnel. Take exit 15, I-264 east. Take exit 7B (Downtown Portsmouth) and follow Crawford Street to North Landing, near the corner of Crawford and North Streets. *By public transportation:* Take Amtrak (1-800-USA-RAIL, www.amtrak.com) or Greyhound (1-800-231-2222, www.greyhound.com) to Norfolk. From the Waterside in Norfolk take the Elizabeth River Ferry (757-222-6100) to North Landing.

Named for the English port and city, Portsmouth was founded in 1752. Just 15 years later, in 1767, a shipyard was built here, which became the Norfolk Navy Yard in 1801. In 1861 the Navy Yard was seized by Confederate forces. The Confederates, using the hull of the U.S.S. *Merrimack,* built the ironclad *Virginia.* Today the facility is known as the Norfolk Naval Shipyard and remains a vital part of the area's economy.

This walk begins at **North Landing (1).** Walk to Crawford Street and stop at the **statue (2)** dedicated

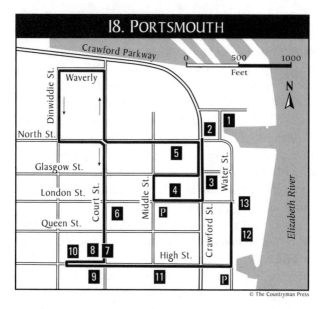

18. PORTSMOUTH

Crawford Parkway

Dinwiddie St.

Waverly

North St.

Glasgow St.

Court St.

London St.

Middle St.

Queen St.

High St.

Water St.

Crawford St.

Elizabeth River

0   500   1000

Feet

N

© The Countryman Press

to those who fought in the Philippines and Cuba during the Spanish-American War. Continue along Crawford Street. On the left (near Glasgow Street) you will see the **Lafayette Arch (3).** Built in 1976, the arch commemorates the visit of the Marquis de Lafayette to Portsmouth in 1824. Turn right onto London Street. Number **218–220 London Street (4)** was a tavern in the mid-18th century. Turn right onto Middle Street, and then right onto Glasgow Street, returning to Crawford Street. From Crawford turn left onto North Street and stop at the **Hill House (5),** at 221 North. This is a fine example of an English basement house—the basement is actually built above ground level. Captain John Thompson built the Hill House in about 1820. The captain's nephew, John Thompson Hill, later acquired the house. Lived in by generations of the Hill family for nearly a century and a half, the house is filled with family furnishings and memorabilia and is now open to the public (757-393-5111).

Continue up North Street to Court Street. Turn right onto Court Street and circle the block, turning left onto Waverly, left onto Dinwiddie, and left onto North, returning to Court Street. Walk south on Court Street. On your left, at the corner of Court and Queen Streets, stands the massive granite Romanesque Revival **Court Street Baptist Church (6),** built early in the 20th century. Its congregation was founded in 1789.

Farther along Court Street you will see the **Confederate War Memorial (7).** An immense, towering monument, it took five years to build, from 1876 to 1881. The four statues at the monument's base represent the Confederate military: Navy, Infantry, Calvary, and Artillery.

Continue on Court Street to the intersection of High Street. This juncture was planned as the town square when Portsmouth was founded in 1752, its four corners the sites of the courthouse, church, jail, and market. Look at the redbrick, Greek Revival **courthouse (8)** on the right. Built in 1846, this is on the National Register of Historic Places. Now it houses the Courthouse Galleries, a museum devoted to "offering quality educational, cultural, and aesthetic experiences in the arts through rotating visual art exhibits, lectures, classes, and performances. Local, national, and international themes are represented, as well as craftsmen and artists of various genres. Classical to contemporary, mainstream to the fringe, this museum promotes the interest and understanding of visual fine art" (757-393-8543, www.courthousegalleries.com).

Trinity Episcopal Church (9), Portsmouth's oldest church building, stands opposite the courthouse. It was built the same year the parish was founded, 1762. The original brick facade has since been covered with stucco, and the church was enlarged in 1828 and again in 1894. The bell hanging here dates to colonial times and earned a crack while pealing in celebration of the British surrender at Yorktown on October 19, 1781. Many Revolutionary War patriots are buried in the church's graveyard (757-383-0431).

The **Virginia Sports Hall of Fame and Museum (10)** is just a few doors away at 420 High Street. Sports legends from Virginia are featured here, including Sam Snead and Arthur Ashe (757-393-8031).

Walk down High Street toward the Elizabeth River. The **Children's Museum of Virginia (11)** will be on the right at 221 High Street. The museum has over 90 hands-on exhibits and a collection of toy trains bound to impress and entertain children of all ages (757-393-8393, www.childrensmuseumva.com).

Continue down High Street. Turn left onto Water Street and the **Portsmouth Naval Shipyard Museum (12)** will be on the right. The history of America's oldest and largest naval shipyard is illustrated here through exhibits of ship models, uniforms, and other military artifacts. Additionally, there are permanent exhibits about life in Portsmouth in the 1700s and 1800s (757-393-8591, www.portsva.com).

Your next stop is the **Lightship Museum (13).** Since 1820 lightships have functioned as floating lighthouses, the lanterns atop their masts safely guiding vessels to shore. The lightship *Portsmouth* was commissioned in 1915, designated a National Historic Landmark in

1989, is now permanently docked here, and is opened to the public as a museum in which models, uniforms, photos, and other artifacts are exhibited (757-393-8741, www.portsva.com).

Continue along the waterfront, returning to North Landing where this tour began.

19 · Charlottesville

Directions: *By car:* From the Capital Beltway take I-66 to Warrenton, Virginia. Then take US 29 to Charlottesville and follow the signs to the University of Virginia Rotunda. *By public transportation:* Greyhound (1-800-231-2222, www.greyhound.com) and Amtrak (1-800-USA-RAIL, www.amtrak.com) have service between Washington and Charlottesville.

Charlottesville was named for Queen Charlotte, consort of King George III. At first settled as a tobacco trading center in 1730, the town became the Albemarle county seat in 1761. To many Charlottesville is synonymous with Thomas Jefferson. He was born in Albemarle County, spent much of his life here, built his beloved home Monticello overlooking the city, founded Charlottesville's most famous institution, the University of Virginia, and died here on July 4th, 1826. Two local men, Capt. Meriwether Lewis and Lt. William Clark, were sent by Jefferson from Charlottesville in 1803 to explore the American West.

This tour begins at Charlottesville's best-known landmark: **the Rotunda (1)** at the University of Virginia. When he founded the school in 1819, Jefferson envisioned an "academical village," with the Rotunda, housing the library, at the core. Jefferson's model and

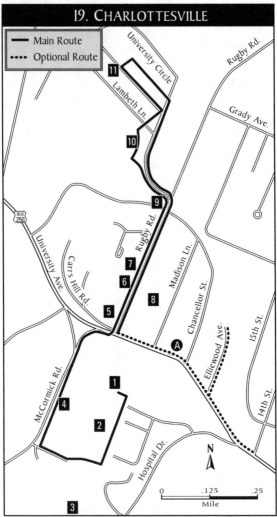

19. CHARLOTTESVILLE

Main Route
Optional Route

University Circle

Rugby Rd.

11

Lambeth Ln.

Grady Ave.

10

BUS 250

9

University Ave.

Rugby Rd.

7

Carrs Hill Rd.

6

Madison Ln.

8

Chancellor St.

15th St.

5

A

Elliewood Ave.

14th St.

1

McCormick Rd.

4

2

Hospital Dr.

N

0   .125   .25
Mile

© The Countryman Press

inspiration for the Rotunda was the 2nd-century Roman temple known as the Pantheon. Enter the Rotunda through a basement-level passageway under the main stairs facing the Lawn. Note the interior floor plan: an hourglass-shaped central hall flanked by two oval rooms. The plan is repeated on the second floor, and above that is the dome room. The Rotunda was burned in a devastating fire in 1895; only the outer shell of the building remained. Stanford White redesigned and embellished the Rotunda, reflecting the beaux-arts style so popular at that time. In the 1930s the ever-growing library collection was moved to another hall. In 1973 the Rotunda was restored to look as it did in Jefferson's day. On the interior stairway pause to look at the Lawn, surrounded by Jefferson's academical village. The American Institute of Architects has declared this the most significant American architectural achievement in the last two centuries. The students at the desk by the door will answer questions, provide literature, and offer guided tour information (434-924-7969, www.virginia. edu/academicalvillage).

Return to the whitewashed basement-level outdoor corridor, turn left, and walk a few steps until you see the columned walkway on the right that borders **the Lawn (2).** Turn right, walking past students' rooms and pavilions. Jefferson placed 10 architecturally distinctive pavilions on both sides of the Lawn. Faculty lived upstairs; classrooms were downstairs.

At the end of the colonnade turn right and cross the Lawn, stopping midway to admire the Rotunda. Opposite the Rotunda stands **Cabell Hall (3),** designed by McKim, Mead, and White about a century ago. These additions enclosed the Lawn, which had been open to the surrounding countryside. Though lamented by some, the halls block views of what has become a residential neighborhood.

Continue across the Lawn, past the Pavilion Gardens, and turn right at the outer (or range) walkway which parallels McCormick Road. You are now at the West Range. The ranges have more students' rooms. These are punctuated with hotels in which students dined. Room number 31 was lived in by student Woodrow Wilson. Stop at **Edgar Allan Poe's (4),** room number 13. Poe was born in 1809 and was a student here in 1826. Inspired by the Blue Ridge Mountains, he wrote *A Tale of the Ragged Mountains.* Push the button to hear an audio presentation about Poe and his life at the university. His room is maintained by the Raven Society.

Face McCormick Road and turn right. On the left will be the newly completed Harrison Institute and Small Library, which houses the special collections library and its changing exhibits of rare books, manuscripts, and other artifacts. The exterior statue of a winged young man was modeled in 1918 by James R. McConnell.

The Gothic Revival chapel before you was built between 1884 and 1890. Cross University Avenue in back of the chapel. On the left is **Carr's Hill (5),** the official residence of UVA's president. The hill got its name from Mrs. Sidney S. Carr, who opened a student boardinghouse here in 1854. In 1864 she sold the property to the university and a dormitory replaced the boardinghouse. Then in 1907 the firm of McKim, Mead, and White was commissioned to design the Southern Colonial Revival president's house you see here today.

ROBERT J. REGALBUTO

Jefferson's "academical village" at the University of Virginia

Furnished with fine antiques, paintings, portraits, and other artwork, Carr's Hill receives about 15,000 visitors each year at presidential meetings, parties, and special occasions.

From University Avenue walk straight down Rugby Road. **Fayerweather Hall (6)** will be on the left. Daniel B. Fayerweather, a New Yorker who made his fortune in the shoe industry, funded the building of gymnasia at several colleges. This is one of them. Built in 1892, Fayerweather filled a void in the school's facilities, providing its first gymnasium. No longer used for athletics, Fayerweather Hall now houses the university's McIntire Department of Art and its galleries display students' artwork.

Next on the left is the **University of Virginia Art Museum (7).** Completed in 1935, the building was a gift of Mrs. Evelyn May Bayly Tiffany. Note the entrance portico, which reflects a signature design of the 16th-century Italian architect Andrea Palladio. A Palladian window usually consists of a large, central, round-topped window flanked by two smaller rectangular ones. Here Palladio's window has been translated for use on a portico. Visit the museum's galleries. There are plans to extend the university's fine-arts facilities farther along Rugby Road (434-924-3592, www.virginia. edu/artmuseum).

When you leave the museum look straight across the street to **Madison Bowl (8),** the sunken athletic playing field also known as Mad Bowl. The building to the right of the bowl is Madison Hall. Built in 1904, it housed a chapter of the YMCA. Now owned by the university, Madison Hall is used for office space. At the far side of Mad Bowl is a parade of fraternity and sorority houses, most of which were built in the first quarter of the twentieth century.

Resume your walk on Rugby Road and cross **Beta Bridge (9),** so-called because the Beta Theta fraternity once had a house here. Note the Westminster Presbyterian Church on the right. Built in 1939, it is a Colonial Revival design inspired by the parish church in Abington, Virginia. The church houses an exceptionally fine organ modeled on 17th-century German instruments.

Once over the bridge make an immediate left onto University Way, which will lead you to the **Lambeth Colonnade (10).** Built in 1913 in imitation of a classical amphitheater, the colonnade today no longer overlooks an athletic playing field, but dormitories built on the field. Directly in front of you in the distance, the building with the shallow, umbrella-like dome is University Hall. Built in 1965 to accommodate UVA's indoor athletics, U Hall was inspired by the Palazzo dello Sport, designed by Pier Luigi Nervi for the

Olympics held in Rome in 1960. To the left of U Hall is Lewis Mountain, which is crowned by a house built in 1909 by Eugene Bradbury for John Watts Kearney. To the right of University Hall are splendid views of the Blue Ridge Mountains.

Walk along the colonnade a bit farther and turn right, climbing the slight hill back to Rugby Road. Then turn left onto University Circle. Stop at **35 University Circle (11),** which was the home to royalty (or purported royalty)—Anna Anderson who claimed to be the Grand Duchess Anastasia, a daughter of Czar Nicholas II, Russia's last reigning monarch. She immigrated to America in 1968, married UVA faculty member John E. Manahan, and lived in this house until she died in 1984, insisting to the end that she was Anastasia. Ten years later British scientists retrieved a sample of Mrs. Manahan's tissue from a Charlottesville laboratory and performed a DNA test. At the same time a DNA sample was taken from Prince Philip who is related to the Romanovs through his grandmother (who was a sister of Empress Alexandra). They did not match; Mrs. Manahan was not the Grand Duchess Anastasia. Professor Manahan is also dead, and the house is lived in by another family today.

Retrace your steps to Rugby Road and then to University Avenue. The north side of the Rotunda faces University Avenue. A long, rectangular, shoe box–shaped wing extending almost to the street was added to the Rotunda in 1853. The 1895 Rotunda fire started in this wing. The present appearence of the north side of the Rotunda today is largely the work of Stanford White.

Option A: You may want to continue to walk along University Avenue to The Corner, the University's restaurant, retail, and entertainment area. Elliewood Avenue, a charming cul-de-sac with specialty shops and eateries, will be on the left. On the right will be the University of Virginia Hospital, which has its roots in Jefferson's Anatomical Theatre. Christopher Reeve, recovering from his 1995 equestrian accident in the Virginia countryside, received his initial care here. University Avenue meets West Main Street, which leads to Charlottesville's downtown area. In colonial times this stretch was known as Three Notch Road, the main thoroughfare in the wilderness, connecting The University with the town of Charlottesville and Richmond beyond.

Also Nearby

Monticello, Thomas Jefferson's House (434-984-9800, www.monticello.org)

Ash Lawn Highland, James Monroe's house (434-293-9539, http://monticello.avenue.org/ash-lawn)

Mitchie Tavern (434-977-1234, www.mitchietavern.com)

20 · Lexington

Directions: *By car:* From the Capital Beltway take I-66 west to I-81 south. Take exit 188B to US 60 west. Drive 3 miles, following the blue-and-white signs to the information center. At the fourth traffic light turn right onto Lewis Street, which becomes Washington Street. The information center parking lot is on the right. *By public transportation:* Greyhound (1-800-231-2222, www.greyhound. com) has bus service to Buena Vista, Virginia. It is then a 5-mile cab ride to Lexington. Call in advance to be met by a taxi: Dunn's Taxi Service (540-463-1056), Franks's Cab Co. (540-464-3198), or Rockbridge Taxi Service (540-261-7733).

Lexington was founded in 1777, burned in 1796, and rose from the ashes to become the picturesque university town it is today. Start your tour in the historic downtown area at the **visitors center (1),** 106 East Washington Street at the corner of Randolph Street. Cross Washington Street to the **Rockbridge Historical Society (2),** located in the Campbell House. Built as an elegant home for a local innkeeper, the house includes a museum with permanent and changing exhibits illustrating local history (540-464-1058,

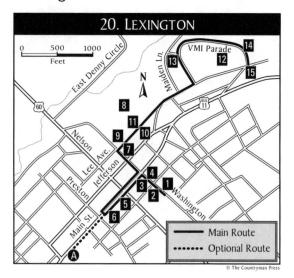

© The Countryman Press

www.rockhist.org/rockbridge.htm).

Cross Randolph Street and walk along Washington Street. As you approach the redbrick and Kentucky bluestone **courthouse (3),** built in 1897, lawyer's row will be on the left. On the right, at 8 East Washington Street, is the **Stonewall Jackson House (4).** Gen. Thomas J. "Stonewall" Jackson lived here from 1858 to 1861, while on the faculty of the Virginia Military Institute in town. He left to fight in the Civil War. The house, built in 1801 and completely restored in 1979, is open to the public, as is its garden. Tours are given (540-463-2552, www.stonewalljackson.org).

Turn left onto Main Street and cross Nelson Street. The **Lexington Presbyterian Church (5)** will be on the left. Stonewall Jackson was an active member. Built in 1845, this Greek Revival church was destroyed by a fire in 2000 and is being rebuilt.

The brick walkway next to the Presbyterian church leads to what may be Lexington's best kept secret. The **Museum of Military Memorabilia (6),** at 122½ South Main Street, displays a private collection of uniforms and other military artifacts. Gathered from the United States, Great Britain, Europe, and Asia, the collection spans the period from the 1740s to the present (540-464-3041).

Option A: To visit the burial place of Stonewall Jackson and his family, walk two blocks south on Main Street. The cemetery entrance gate will be on the left. The statue of Jackson was modeled by the well-known Richmond sculptor Edward Valentine and dedicated in 1891. The cemetery is the site of the first Lexington Presbyterian Church, built in 1789.

Return to Washington Street and turn left. The **Robert E. Lee Memorial Episcopal Church (7)** will be on the right. Lee approved the plans for this church in 1870, just a few days before he died. The church was completed in 1883 (540-463-4981).

You are now surrounded by the campus of **Washington and Lee University (8)** (540-463-8400, www.wlu.edu). Founded in 1749, the school was named Augusta Academy and later known as Liberty Hall Academy (1776). In 1796 George Washington saved the academy from closing by donating a substantial sum to its endowment. The school was then renamed in his honor. Retired General Robert E. Lee was the university's president for a mere five years, from 1865 to 1870, but in that brief period established the nation's first school of journalism, founded the university's law school, and set in place its honor system. The general died in 1870, and the following year the school was

ROBERT J. REGALBUTO

Washington and Lee University

renamed Washington and Lee University.

Just beyond the church follow the path to the right. Look across the lawn on the left. The first house in the row is the **Lee House (9).** Built for the general in 1869, it remains the university president's official residence. The next house to its right is the Lee-Jackson House, built in 1842. Stonewall Jackson married Elinor Junkin, the university president's daughter, in this house in 1853. The couple then lived in the house for a time. The last house in the row of three is another faculty house, also built in 1842.

Follow the path across Front Campus to the **Lee Chapel (10).** The chapel was built for the university under Lee's direction in 1867. Step inside. Robert E. Lee and some of his family are buried in the crypt. The statue of the Recumbent Lee was sculpted by the well-respected artist and Virginian Edward Valentine. (Valentine's studio is a stop on the Richmond tour, see page 116.) Coincidentally, the two generals who aided WLU, Washington and Lee, were related by marriage. The chapel's museum displays works of art belonging to the Washington, Custis, and Lee families, including a portrait of George Washington by Charles Wilson Peale. The office used by Robert E. Lee while university president may also be visited in the chapel. It remains just as he left it. Lee's famous and beloved horse, Traveller, is buried just a few steps from his master, in a marked grave outside the chapel walls (540-463-8768, http://leechapel.wlu.edu).

On leaving the chapel turn your attention to the rambling redbrick Greek Revival collegiate hall faced with rows of white columns and pilasters. In the center is **Washington Hall (11),** built in 1824. It is flanked by Payne Hall on the left and Robinson Hall on the right. Know collectively as Washington College, these and the chapel are National Historic Landmarks. Note the statue of George Washington atop the cupola. The present bronze statue replaces the 1844 original.

Continue on the path, walking toward Letcher Avenue. Cross Maiden Lane and walk to the Parade of the **Virginia Military Institute (12).** Founded in 1839, the campus of this 4-year college is a National Historic District. Start your visit at a memorial dedicated to one of VMI's alumni, General George C. Marshall. Turn left at the Parade and the **George C. Marshall Museum (13)** will be on the left. Born in Pennsylvania in 1880, Marshall graduated from VMI in 1901 and began a distinguished career as a soldier-statesman, serving as U.S. Army chief of staff, ambassador to China, secretary of state, secretary of defense, author of the Marshall Plan, and Nobel Peace Prize recipient. He died in 1959. (Dodona Manor, his home and retreat, is a stop on the Leesburg tour; see page 96.) In 1964 this museum, library, and archive was dedicated to General Marshall (540-463-7103, www.marshallfoundation.org).

On the opposite side of the Parade are the **VMI Barracks (14),** built in 1851. The statue of Stonewall Jackson depicts the general surveying the battlefield at Chancellorsville, Virginia, during the Civil War. The cannons on either side of Jackson were used by the general as tools when he taught at VMI.

Walk to **Jackson Memorial Hall** and the **VMI Cadet Museum (15).** The museum displays hundreds of VMI artifacts and those of its most distinguished alumni, including George Patton and Richard E. Byrd. You may see the coat Stonewall Jackson was wearing when he was mortally wounded. Also, the general's horse is preserved, mounted, and displayed (404-464-7334, www.vmi.edu/museum).

The walking tour ends at the museum. To return to the visitors center, follow Letcher Avenue back to town.

21 · Appomattox Court House

Directions: *By car:* From the Capital Beltway take I-66 to I-81 south to Lexington. From Lexington take US 60 east to Bent Creek, then VA 26 south to Appomattox. Turn left onto VA 24 and drive 3 miles. The Appomattox Court House National Historic Park Visitor Center will be on the left. *By public transportation:* Greyhound (1-800-231-2222, www.greyhound.com) has limited service to the town of Appomattox. From town it is a 3-mile walk or cab ride to the National Historic Park.

Appomattox Court House, "where our nation was reunited," is a cluster of homes, law offices, and small businesses that grew around this county seat in rural Virginia. At first a stagecoach stop and tavern surrounded by a hamlet on the road between Richmond and Lynchburg, it was known as Clover Hill. Appomattox County, an area of rolling hills and farmland with no towns, was formed in 1845. The county seat was placed here and named, appropriately, Appomattox Court House. Twenty years later, when the village earned its place in history as the spot where Lee surrendered to Grant, the community had grown to include 150 people.

Following the surrender in 1865, Appomattox Court

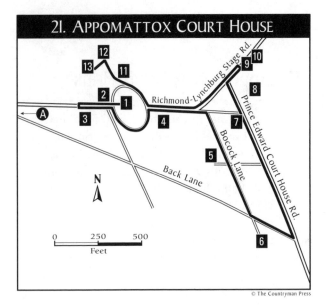

21. APPOMATTOX COURT HOUSE

© The Countryman Press

House declined. The court was moved in 1895, and the remaining buildings either burned, decayed, or were abandoned. In 1935 the National Park Service initiated the rebuilding and restoration of the site. Today Appomattox Court House National Historic Park, a village of 27 buildings surrounded by 1,744 protected acres, is open to visitors (434-352-8797, www.nps.gov/apco).

The park's **visitors center (1)** is located in the restored courthouse. Built in 1846, the original courthouse was destroyed by fire in 1892, and the county seat moved to the town of Appomattox. Rebuilt by the National Park Service in 1965, this is an excellent place to start your visit, pay your entry fee, and begin your orientation through the center's exhibits and audio-visual presentation.

Robert E. Lee surrendered to Ulysses S. Grant on Palm Sunday, April 9, 1865. The courthouse was closed that day, and the meeting took place at the McLean House, which you will visit later on this walk. When you leave the courthouse walk straight down the Richmond-Lynchburg Stage Road in front of you. The **Plunkett-Meeks Store (2)** stands opposite the front door of the courthouse. Built by John Plunkett in 1852, it was later owned by merchant, druggist, and postmaster Francis Meeks. It then became a Presbyterian minister's house, or manse. The small frame building in back of the store is the Woodson Law Office, which was built in the early 1850s.

As you walk along the Richmond-Lynchburg Stage Road, follow the white fence on the left to the **McLean House (3),** where Generals Lee and Grant met on April 9, 1865. The house was built in 1848 and bought fifteen years later, in 1863, by Wilmer McLean. Ironically, McLean moved here with his family to escape the violence and destruction of the Civil War; his previous home was near the site of the Battle of Bull Run in Manasses, Virginia. Following Lee's surrender souvenir collectors took what they could from the house. The destruction was completed in 1893 when the building was dismantled for transport to Washington, D.C., where it was to be reconstructed as a museum. The house never made the journey, and its bricks and timbers were but a decaying pile of rubble until rescued by the National Park Service. Now rebuilt, the house's dependencies include the well (enclosed in a gazebo on the front lawn), an ice house, the kitchen, slave quarters, and a privy.

Option A: Continue along Stage Road about a quarter mile until you arrive at the Confederate Cemetery. Then reverse direction, pass the courthouse, and continue the main tour.

Return to the courthouse, walk to the back on the circular road, and continue straight ahead on the Richmond-Lynchburg Stage Road. The **Appomattox County Jail (4)** will be on the right. Begun in 1860, the jail was not completed until 1870. The sheriff had his office and living quarters on the first floor; the prisoners' cells were above. The original county jail stood across the road. An original structure, the jail has been restored.

Continue along the road. On the left, beyond the site of the first jail, once stood a house and shops. At the fork in the road bear right, and then turn right onto Babcock Lane. The white clapboard house on the right is the **Babcock-Isbell House (5).** Built in 1849 for two brothers—Thomas Babcock, speaker of the Confederate Congress, and Henry Babcock, the local clerk of the court—the house was completed in 1865. It is not open to visitors.

As you continue along Babcock Lane the **Mariah Wright House (6)** will be directly in front of you. Her house dates to the 1820s, and its stone-and-brick end-chimneys are characteristic of houses of this region and period. It is not open to visitors.

Turn left onto Back Lane, and left again onto Prince Edward Court House Road. The **Jones Law Office (7),** built before 1860, is ahead on the left. Crawford Jones used this as his in-town home and office.

Continue to walk to the end of Prince Edward Court House Road. The clapboard house you pass on the right is known as the **Peers House (8).** Built before 1855, it has had several owners. It is not open to visitors.

ROBERT J. REGALBUTO

McLean House

At the **T** intersection turn right onto the Richmond-Lynchburg Stage Road. Stop at the **fork in the road (9).** It was here on April 10, 1865, that Generals Lee and Grant had their second meeting. Just a few feet away, **(10),** Joshua Lawrence Chamberlain, a Union general from Maine, and John Brown Gordon, a Confederate general from Georgia, saluted each other during the Ceremony of Surrender on April 12, 1865.

Reverse your direction and walk along the Richmond-Lynchburg Stage Road. From this point to the courthouse and then beyond as far as the McLean House the Stacking of Arms took place on April 12. Confederate soldiers lined the road with their arms and battle flags.

As you approach the courthouse, circle the visitors center to the right. The **Clover Hill Tavern (11)** is on the right. The oldest building here, it was built in 1819 when Clover Hill was a budding settlement. The tavern played a role in the surrender: Printing presses were set up here which produced 30,000 blank paroles. The forms were then completed in pen and ink for each Confederate soldier.

The Clover Hill Tavern was a place for food, libation, and rest. Visit the dependencies in back of the tavern. The **tavern kitchen (12)** has been converted for use as a bookshop, and the slave quarters next to it now houses restrooms. The **tavern guesthouse (13)** accommodated the overflow of travelers when the tavern rooms were fully booked.

You have come full circle and returned to the courthouse.

Option B: The National Park Service's hiking trail will lead you to the site of General Grant's headquarters at one end of the park, and to the site of General Lee's headquarters at the opposite end. If you plan to take the hike, be sure to pick up a map at the visitors center.

III. Maryland

22 · Baltimore: Mount Vernon Place

Directions: *By car:* From I-95 take exit 53 to I-395 north. Continue north on Howard Street and turn right onto Centre Street. The Washington Monument is 1 block north of the intersection of Centre and Charles Streets. *By public transportation:* Rail service between Washington and Baltimore is provided by Amtrak (1-800-USA-RAIL, www.amtrak.com) and MARC (1-800-325-RAIL, www.mtamaryland.com). Bus service is provided by Greyhound (1-800-231-2222, www.greyhound.com) and by Peter Pan Bus (1-800-343-9999, www.peterpan-bus.com). Within Baltimore, take the Light Rail to the Centre Street stop (410-539-5000, 1-800-RIDE-MTA, www.mtamaryland.com).

We know that Captain John Smith, exploring the Chesapeake Bay in 1608, visited what is now Baltimore's harbor. In 1661, David Jones established the first plantation in this area. By the 1720s the tobacco growers here needed a shipping port, and so Baltimore Town was founded and a port opened in 1729. Maryland's governor was Benedict Leonard Calvert, Lord Baltimore, and the town was named for his Irish barony.

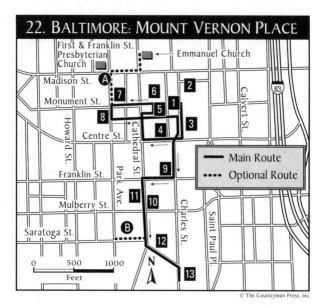

22. BALTIMORE: MOUNT VERNON PLACE

First & Franklin St. Presbyterian Church
Emmanuel Church
Madison St.
Monument St.
Howard St.
Centre St.
Cathedral St.
Park Ave.
Franklin St.
Mulberry St.
Saratoga St.
Charles St.
Saint Paul Pl.
Calvert St.
83

— Main Route
···· Optional Route

0   500   1000
Feet
N

© The Countryman Press, Inc.

This guide has four distinctive self-guided walks in Baltimore, and the city's history and heritage unfolds on each tour. Begin at the **Washington Monument (1).** In the early 19th century this was a wooded hill on the outskirts of town overlooking the harbor. In 1815, John Eager Howard donated the hilltop to build this, the nation's first major monument to George Washington. Robert Mills designed the monument. He later went on to design another memorial to George Washington: the obelisk on the Mall in Washington, D.C. It took 14 years to build this memorial. The 178-foot monument is topped by a 16½-foot statue of Washington that was sculpted by the Italian artist Enrico Causici, whose work also embellishes the nation's Capitol. Step inside the chamber at the monument's base. An exhibit relates the story of Mount Vernon and its monument. You may also climb 220 steps to enjoy a bird's-eye view of the square.

John Eager Howard's descendants further developed the hilltop by laying out gardens east and west, north and south, creating the cross-shaped park you see today. North of the Washington Monument is an equestrian statue of John Eager Howard. Starting in the 1840s and for a century following Mount Vernon Place was Baltimore's most desirable address. Facing north, **Mount Vernon Place United Methodist Church (2)** is on the right. Built in 1872 (Dixon and Carson, architects), this is a Victorian Gothic Revival design, its permanent polychrome achieved through the use of local gray-green serpentine and brown sandstones.

Facing south, the **Peabody Institute (3)** will be on the left. Its two-story Renaissance Revival exterior belies what is within: a six-story atrium. It is considered one of the most dramatic interior architectural spaces in the city.

Still facing south, the **Walters Art Museum (4)** is to the right; the entrance is around the block on Centre Street near the corner of Cathedral Street. William T. Walters (1820–1894) began the nucleus of this collection in the 1840s. At first acquiring works by local artists, he moved to Paris during the Civil War and expanded his collection to include works by French artists. He also collected Chinese ceramics. After the war Walters displayed much of his collection in his Baltimore mansion. The art galley he built in 1908, a magnificent replica of the Genoese Palazzo Balbi, was designed by William Delano. William T. Walter's son, Henry, expanded his father's collection, both in number of objects and in scope. Henry gave the palazzo and its collection to Baltimore in 1931. A wing was added in 1974, and the palazzo has been restored and the adjacent Hackerman House opened. Today the Walters collection encompasses artwork from 55 centuries. Thomas Hoving, past director of New York's Metropolitan Museum of Art, has declared the Walters, "piece for piece, the best art museum in the entire United States." In addition to the galleries there is a library, a shop, and a cafe. (410-547-9000, www.thewalters.org).

On leaving the museum turn right, then right onto Cathedral Street and right onto Mount Vernon Place. Look at number 7–11 on the right, the **Garrett House (5).** A Stanford White design, it was built for B & O Railroad president Robert Garrett in 1884. After Mrs. Garrett was widowed she married Dr. Henry Barton Jacobs, hired architect John Russell Pope, and had the house doubled in size. Work was completed in 1905. The Grand Dame of Baltimore Society, Mrs. Jacobs entertained lavishly. She died in 1936. Now owned by the Engineering Society of Baltimore, the house is open to visitors by appointment (410-539-6914).

On the opposite side of the park is the **Mount Vernon Club (6),** at number 8 Mount Vernon Place. Built in 1842, a century later this Greek Revival townhouse became a private women's club.

Reverse direction and walk west. At the end of the park jog to the right just a few steps and walk along Monument Street. **Grace and St. Peter's Church (7)** will be on the right at the corner of Park Avenue. Built in 1852, it successfully mimics an English country church. The building and its interior appointments reflect this Episcopal parish's Anglo-Catholic heritage, where high

© BACVA, RICHARD NOWITZ, PHOTOGRAPHER

The Washington Monument, Mount Vernon Place

mass, incense, Elizabethan English, and English cathedral music are cherished (410-539-1935, www.grace-andstpeter.org).

Option A: Two more outstanding Gothic Revival churches are close by. Walk north on Park Avenue just 1 block to Madison Street and the First and Franklin Street Presbyterian Church. The oldest Presbyterian congregation in Baltimore, First Presbyterian was founded in 1761. (Franklin Street Presbyterian merged with it in 1973.) Its first worship space was a simple log meetinghouse. This church building was begun in 1855.

Both its exterior and interior are remarkable. The spire is the tallest church tower in the city, rising 273 feet. The interior is a vast expanse without pillars; the plaster-work is considered the finest in the country (410-728-5545, www.firstfranklin.org).

Facing the church, turn right onto Madison Street and then left onto Cathedral Street. Emmanuel Episcopal Church will be on the right. Built in 1854, the church was expanded and embellished in the early 20th century. The Flemish Gothic belfry is known as the Christmas Tower, because of its sculpture. The interior has many treasures by noted artists and artisans: the baptismal font by Daniel Chester French (who modeled the seated president at Washington's Lincoln Memorial), stained-glass windows by Tiffany and John LaFarge, and high-altar reredos carved by the renowned Johannes Kirschmayer (410-685-1130, www.emmanuelepisco-palchurch.org).

Baltimore journalist and literary critic H.L. Mencken lived for a short time with his wife at 704 Cathedral Street.

The walk resumes at the corner of Park Avenue and Monument Street. The **Maryland Historical Society (8)** is at 201 West Monument. Founded in 1844, the society's outstanding collection includes Francis Scott Key's original manuscript for "The Star-Spangled Banner," an extensive art collection with many works by Maryland artist Charles Wilson Peale, maritime memorabilia, and military artifacts from the American Revolution, the War of 1812, and the Civil War—over five million objects in all. The society also has a library and shop (410-685-3750, www.mdha.org).

Return to the Washington Monument. Turn right,

and walk down Charles Street 2 blocks to Franklin Street. The **First Unitarian Church (9)** will be on the right, built in 1818 by Maximilian Godefroy. The sculpture over the door was first modeled by Antonio Capellano, who also sculpted Baltimore's Battle Monument (see page 203 of this guide). Weatherworn, the original sculpture was replaced by this replica in 1954 (410-685-2330).

Turn right onto Franklin Street and then left onto Cathedral Street. The **Basilica of the Assumption of the Blessed Virgin Mary (10),** the first Roman Catholic cathedral in America, will be on the left. It was inspired by the late 18th-century Neoclassical Panthéon built in Paris. Many modifications were made, such as the long nave and the curious towers and spires flanking the portico. Ironically, the two onion domes are among the basilica's most distinctive features, and yet it is doubtful that these were intended by the cathedral's architect, Benjamin H. Latrobe. The basilica's cornerstone was laid in 1806, and the building was dedicated in 1821. In 1995 it was visited by Pope John Paul II (410-727-3565, www.baltimorebasilica.org).

Facing the basilica is the **Enoch Pratt Free Library (11).** Pratt was a wealthy merchant who endowed the city with a library constructed just around the corner on Mulberry Street in 1886. It was replaced with the present limestone building in 1933, and has grown to include 28 branches and 300,000 members. The papers and personal library of Baltimore journalist and literary critic H.L. Mencken are a part of the collection. On display are a collection of full-length portraits of the Lords Baltimore given to the library by well-respected John Hopkins Medical School surgeon Dr. Hugh Hampton

Young (410-396-5430, www.pratt.lib.md.us/).

Facing the basilica's front door, turn right and walk down Cathedral Street to Saratoga Street.

Option B: St. Alphonsus Roman Catholic Church may be reached by turning right onto Saratoga Street. Robert Cary Long was the architect for this, Baltimore's first Gothic Revival building, built in 1841. The Gothic details were borrowed from both German and English sources.

The main tour resumes at the corner of Cathedral and Saratoga Streets. Facing the harbor, turn left onto Saratoga Street. **St. Paul's Rectory (12)** will be on the left. On land once owned by John Eager Howard, this Federal house was built in 1789 and is one of the oldest buildings in downtown Baltimore. No longer a rectory, it is now used as an office building.

Continue along Saratoga Street. When you reach Charles Street, **St. Paul's Episcopal Church (13)** will be on the right. The parish dates to 1729, when its first church was built on this site. The second was a Robert Cary Long Sr. design completed in 1817; it burned in 1854. Richard Upjohn was chosen to design the present church. His best-known work is Trinity Church, Wall Street in New York. Considered the champion of Gothic Revival architecture in America, St. Paul's is a radical departure from Upjohn's usual work. Here we see a building inspired by Italian Romanesque basilicas. Note the two bas reliefs flanking the rose window. Both are by Antonio Capellano, whose work may also be seen at Baltimore's Battle Monument and, earlier on this tour, at the First Unitarian Church. They were a part of the second church and survived the fire. The church interior is lit by a series of Victorian stained-glass windows, some of which were made in the studios of Louis Comfort Tiffany (410-685-3403).

The next corner is the intersection of Charles and Lexington Streets. Charles Street leads to the Inner Harbor, and Lexington Street leads to city hall, both starting points for other walking tours in this guide book (see "Baltimore: The Inner Harbor" and "Baltimore: City Hall, the Shot Tower, and More").

Also Nearby

Baltimore Museum of Art (410-396-7100)

Evergreen House (410-516-0341)

Johns Hopkins University gardens and museum (410-516-8171)

Lovey Lane Methodist Church (410-889-1512)

23 • Baltimore: The Inner Harbor

Directions: *By car:* From I-95 take exit 53 (I-395 north). Turn right onto Pratt Street. The Inner Harbor will be on your right. *By public transportation:* Rail service between Washington and Baltimore is provided by Amtrak (1-800-USA-RAIL, www.amtrak.com) and MARC (1-800-325-RAIL, www.mtamaryland.com). Bus service is provided by Greyhound (1-800-231-2222, www.greyhound.com) and Peter Pan Bus (1-800-343-9999, www.peterpan-bus.com). Within Baltimore, take the Metro Subway to the Charles Centre stop (410-539-5000, 1-800-RIDE-MTA, www.mtamaryland.com).

Originally known as the Basin, the Inner Harbor was a vital, thriving port from Baltimore's first days up to the 1960s. By then trucks replaced the frigates that once brought in produce and products to the port; highway transportation made commuting by boat a thing of the past. The deteriorating, neglected Inner Harbor was revitalized in 1978 when the Rouse Company initiated Harborplace. A vibrant complex of restaurants and shops housed in the Pratt Street and the Light Street Pavilions, Harborplace has been a success and has expanded to the Gallery. It was the spark which

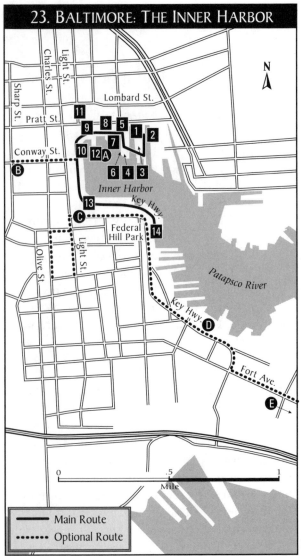

23. BALTIMORE: THE INNER HARBOR

N

Light St.

Charles St.

Sharp St.

Lombard St.

Pratt St.

Conway St.

11

9 8 5 1 2

7

10 12 A

6 4 3

Inner Harbor

Key Hwy.

13

C

Federal Hill Park

14

Olive St.

Light St.

Patapsco River

Key Hwy. D

Fort Ave.

E

0 .5 1

Mile

—— Main Route

······ Optional Route

© The Countryman Press

ignited the redevelopment of the Inner Harbor, which is now home to museums, office space, and more shops and eateries.

Begin at the **Power Plant (1),** the large, redbrick building with the smokestacks on Pier 4, at Pratt Street between Gay Street and Market Place. Once owned by the Baltimore Gas and Electric Company, the plant has been converted for use as a bookshop and restaurant. To enter, walk through one of the smokestacks. Next to the Power Plant, at Pier 5, the **U.S. Coast Guard cutter** *Taney* **(2)** is docked. A National Historic Landmark, the *Taney* is the only warship afloat that survived the Japanese attack on Pearl Harbor on December 7, 1941. Just a few feet away is another National Historic Landmark, the Seven-Foot Knoll Lighthouse, which dates to 1856.

The **Marine Mammal Pavilion (3)** shares Pier 4 with the Power Plant. Opened in 1990, the pavilion showcases several dolphin performances daily in its amphitheater. A footbridge connects the pavilion with the **National Aquarium in Baltimore (4),** on Pier 3. Opened in 1981, it has become one of the city's premier attractions. Both inside and out, a series of large tanks provide living space for a variety of sea creatures. At the very top, inside the glass pyramid, visitors may walk through a re-creation of a verdant tropical jungle populated by birds and other animals (410-576-3800, www.aqua.org).

The **Baltimore Maritime Museum (5)** is next to the aquarium. The museum maintains the *Taney,* seen earlier from Pier 4. Two more vessels, both docked at Pier 3, are also maintained by the museum and are open to visitors. The **U.S. submarine** *Torsk* **(6)** was built in

1944, served in the Pacific, and, with 11,884 dives, has been submerged more times than any other submarine. The **lightship** *Chesapeake* **(7)** first set sail in 1933 and guided craft in the Chesapeake Bay and Delaware Bay for forty years. Tickets to all three vessels are sold at the museum (410-396-3453, www.baltomaritimemuseum.org/).

Having seen some of Baltimore and its Inner Harbor at eye level, try a bird's-eye view. Enter the **World Trade Building (8)** and take the elevator to the Top of the World observation level. The pentagonal tower, built in 1968 and desined by I. M. Pei, rises to a height of 423 feet (410-837-VIEW, www.baltimore.to/topofworld/).

The long, low-lying glass building next to the World Trade Building is the **Pratt Street Pavilion (9).** First opened in 1980 along with the **Light Street Pavilion (10)** (to the right as you face the harbor) the complex has grown to include **the Gallery (11),** which is connected by way of a skywalk. All three buildings combine to form Harborplace, in which there are scores of shops. restaurants, and eateries (410-332-0060, www.harborplace.com).

The **U.S.S.** *Constellation* **(12)** is docked opposite the Pratt Street Pavilion. The last all-sail warship built by the U.S. Navy, the *Constellation* was launched in 1854 and fought in the Civil War. It is open to visitors (410-539-1797, www.constellation.org).

Option A: If you want a respite from walking but would like to see more of the harbor, the Seaport Taxi departs just a few feet to the right of the *Constellation* as you face the port. Tickets are sold at the kiosk. Ask about a special combination ticket that includes the

© BACVA

Baltimore's Inner Harbor

Seaport Taxi and admission to the *Constellation* and the three vessels of the Baltimore Maritime Museum.

Turn left at the corner of the Inner Harbor and walk south.

Option B: The Old Otterbein United Methodist Church, built in 1785, is the oldest church building in Baltimore. The church's congregation was made up of German immigrants, and its belfry houses 18th-century German bells. To reach the church, leave Harborwalk, cross Light Street, and walk west on Conway Street 2 blocks to Sharp Street. Old Otterbein will be on the left (410-685-4703).

It is a short walk along the harbor to the **Maryland Science Center (13).** The center has its roots in the Maryland Academy of Sciences, founded in 1797; this building was completed in 1976. It includes the Davis Planetarium and IMAX Theatre, the Crosby Ramsey Memorial Observatory, dozens of interactive, hands-on exhibits, the Science Store, and a snack bar (410-685-5225, www.mdsci.org).

And now for something completely different: Follow the Harborwalk past Rash Field to the **American Visionary Art Museum (14).** Congress has named this the "national museum, repository, and education center for the best in original, self-taught artistry." From "carved roots to embroidered rags, tattoos to toothpicks, the Visionary transforms dreams, losses, hopes, and ideals into powerful works of art." In addition to seven galleries there are outdoor sculptures, a 55-foot-high Whirligig, the Wildflower Sculpture Garden, a museum shop, and the Joy America Cafe, offering organic cuisine and a roof-top view (410-244-www.avam.org).

Option C: This tour ends at the doorstep of Federal Hill—a delightful old neighborhood filled with restaurants, shops, markets, pubs, and art galleries. Federal Hill Park (next to the American Visionary Art Museum) has tree-shaded benches that face the harbor. From there walk west on Key Highway past the Science Center to Light Street and, beyond that, to Charles Street, where most of the businesses are located. Turn left (south) onto Charles or Light Street and walk to the Cross Street Market, which has been in continual operation since 1846.

Option D: For the hearty walker, Harborwalk continues along Key Highway a half mile to the Baltimore Museum of Industry. Located on a 6-acre campus overlooking the harbor, the museum imaginatively presents the history of technology and its impact on our culture (410-727-4808, www.thebmi.org). Public transportation is available to return to the tour's start.

Option E: It is a farther stretch, about a mile, from the BMI to historic Fort McHenry, at the end of Fort Avenue. Francis Scott Key was inspired to write "The Star

Spangled Banner" when he saw the flag still flying after British bombarded the fort on September 14, 1814. The wooden flagpole is still there on the fort's parade ground. Fort McHenry is a National Monument and Historic Shrine administered by the National Park Service (410-962-4290, www.nps.gov/fomc). Public transportation is available to return to the tour's start.

24 • Baltimore: Railroads, Baseball, and Food

Directions: *By car:* From I-95 take I-395 north and bear right onto Martin Luther King Boulevard. Drive north on the boulevard until you reach Lombard Street. Turn left onto Lombard Street and drive west to Poppleton Street. Turn left onto Poppleton Street and drive south. The entrance gate for the B & O Railroad Museum will be across Pratt Street. *By public transportation:* Rail service between Washington and Baltimore is provided by Amtak (1-800-USA-RAIL, www.amtrak.com) and MARC (1-800-325-RAIL, www.mtamaryland.com). Bus service is provided by Greyhound (1-800-231-2222, www.greyhound.com) and Peter Pan Bus (1-800-343-9999, www.peterpan-bus.com). Within Baltimore, MTA Bus #31 will bring you to the door of the B & O Railroad Museum (1-800-539-5000, www.mtamaryland.com).

This tour begins at the **B & O Railroad Museum (1).** The Baltimore and Ohio Railroad began in 1827 and was the first rail line in America. The museum is located in the Mount Clare Railroad station, which was built in 1829 and is the oldest station in America.

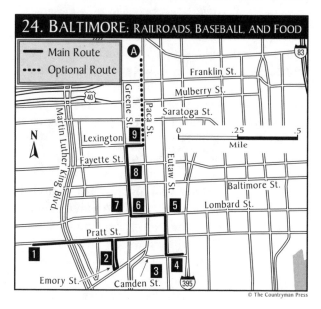

The nucleus of the 40-acre museum campus is the Roundhouse, built in 1884. A former passenger-car shop, it is the world's largest circular industrial building, measuring 235 feet in diameter and 123 feet high. The museum encompasses over 200 major pieces of railroad equipment. Many of the locomotives and cars are permanently housed in the Roundhouse; others are outdoors on tracks. The museum also includes a 12-by-40-foot HO model layout, a shop, and a restaurant (410-752-2490, www.borail.org). *Note:* The Roundhouse roof collapsed during a snowstorm in February, 2003, and restoration is underway.

After visiting the museum walk east along Pratt Street 3 long blocks. The next stop is the **Babe Ruth Birthplace and Museum (2).** From Pratt Street turn right onto Emory Street. The museum will be on the right. George Herman "Babe" Ruth was born at 216 Emory Street on February 6, 1895. A baseball legend, he was also known as the Sultan of Swat and the Bambino. The museum exhibits memorabilia and photographs and gives audio and visual presentations. This is also the official museum of the Baltimore Orioles and Baltimore Colts. Other exhibits focus on Maryland's Negro Leagues, sports journalism, and ballpark architecture (410-727-1539, www.baberuthmuseum.com).

Return to Pratt Street and continue east. Turn right onto Eutaw Street, and the **Oriole Park at Camden Yards (3)** will be on the right. The stadium was completed in 1992. During the excavation, an encampment used by French troops during the American Revolution was discovered. And, interestingly, Babe Ruth has an Oriole Park connection. The Bambino's father once owned a tavern where the park is today. These and other facts are brought to light on park tours. Ballpark Tours tickets are sold at the north end of the Ballpark Warehouse, which is southwest of Camden Station (410-547-6234, www.theorioles.com).

Camden Station (4) stands on the opposite side of Eutaw Street. Built between 1855 and 1867, it was once the city's busiest rail terminal. Closed in 1988, its exterior was restored in 1992. Interior renovations and adaptive reuse are planned.

With your back to the station walk north on Eutaw Street. In the distance you will see the next stop on this tour: the **Bromo Seltzer Tower (5),** at the corner of Eutaw and Lombard Streets. There's a story here. Capt. Isaac E. Emerson founded the Emerson Drug Company, which made Bromo Seltzer. The entrepreneur, on tour in Italy, admired the tower at the Palazzo Vecchio in Florence and had it replicated here in 1911. The surrounding Bromo Seltzer plant is gone, but the tower still stands. It was donated to the city, who renamed it the Baltimore Arts Tower. (A humorous aside: The 300-foot-high tower was once topped with a 50-foot, revolving replica of a Bromo Seltzer bottle!)

Turn left onto Lombard Street and then right onto Greene Street. The **Dr. Samuel D. Harris National Museum of Dentistry (6)** will be on the right. The only museum of its kind, it tells the story of dentistry through lively, interactive exhibits (410-706-0600, www.dentalmuseum.umaryland.edu).

Walk up Greene Street. The campus of the **University of Maryland (7)** will be on the left. Stop at the **Westminster Hall and Burying Ground (8),** at the corner of Greene and Fayette Streets. This land was purchased by a Presbyterian congregation in 1786 for use as a cemetery. It is estimated that there are 1,000 graves in this burying ground, mayors and prominent citizens among them. Undoubtedly the best-known person buried here is Edgar Allan Poe. He died a mysterious death in 1849 at the age of 40, while passing through Baltimore en route from Richmond to New York. In 1852 the church was built over the burying ground. It is supported by brick piers and arches, which transform the burying ground into a kind of catacomb. The church closed in 1977. The Westminster Preservation Trust, Inc. maintains the cemetery and church building today (410-706-2072).

Just 1 1/2 blocks farther up Greene Street is **Lexington Market (9).** In continuous operation since 1782, the market, with over 140 food stalls, is the world's largest fresh-food center. It is also a fitting place to end this tour. Bon appetit!

Option A: Two points of religious interest are 4 blocks north of Lexington Market. The Mother Seton House is at 600 North Paca Street (just beyond Franklin Street). Elizabeth Ann Seton was the first native-born American canonized a saint in the Roman Catholic church. She lived in this house from 1808 to 1809. It is advisable to call for hours before visiting (410-523-3443). Just a few steps beyond the Mother Seton House is the Chapel of Old St. Mary's Seminary. It was built in 1808, and Mother Seton took her vows as a Sister of Charity here in 1809. To reach the house and chapel from Lexington Market, walk east on Saratoga Street 1 block and then turn left, walking 3 blocks north on Paca Street.

Also Nearby

Mount Clare Museum House (410-837-3262)

25 • Baltimore: City Hall, the Old Shot Tower, and More

Directions: *By car:* From I-95 take exit 53(I-395 north). Turn right onto Pratt Street and a left on Calvert Street. *By public transportation:* Rail service between Washington and Baltimore is provided by Amtrak (1-800-USA-RAIL, www.amtrak.com) and MARC (1-800-325-RAIL, www.mtamaryland.com). Bus service is provided by Greyhound (1-800-231-222, www.greyhound.com) and by Peter Pan Bus (1-800-343-9999, www.peterpan-bus.com). Within Baltimore, take the Metro Subway to the Charles Centre stop (410-539-5000, 1-800-RIDE-MTA, www.mtamaryland.com).

Begin your walk at **Battle Monument (1),** on Calvert Street between Fayette and Lexington Streets. Built in 1815 as a memorial to all who died in the British bombardment of Baltimore during the War of 1812, its designer was a Frenchman, Maximilian Godefroy, who was influenced by the Egyptian Revival architecture which was so popular in Napoleonic France. The shaft of the column resembles Roman fasces, which are bound by a ribbon bearing the names of the dead. The names of three officers also killed are at

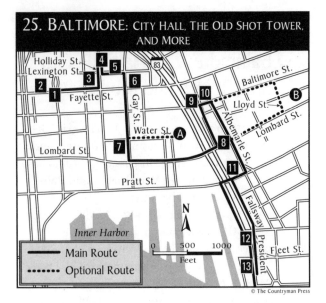

25. BALTIMORE: CITY HALL, THE OLD SHOT TOWER, AND MORE

© The Countryman Press

the top of the column just below the allegorical statue of Baltimore. She holds two symbols in her hands: a rudder (stability) and a laurel wreath (glory). At the base, 18 horizontal bands represent the states in the Union at that time. Overall, the monument stands 40 feet tall. The sculptor was Antonio Capellano.

As you face the monument (with your back to the harbor) the Renaissance Revival **Clarence M. Mitchell Jr. Courthouse (2)** is on the left. It was designed by Wyatt and Nolting and completed in 1900.

Turn right and walk along Fayette Street 2 blocks, then turn left onto Holliday Street. **City Hall (3),** built in 1875, will be on the left. Like so many other city halls' built in that era, including those in Boston, Philadelphia, and Providence, Rhode Island, to name but three, the style used was French Second Empire. The outside walls are 5½ feet thick and are capped with a veneer of marble; the roof and dome are cast iron. Step inside and view the three-story rotunda, which rises to a height of 120 feet (410-396-3100).

Facing city hall turn right and walk up Holliday Street. The **Peale Museum (4)** will be on the right at number 225. It was built by Rembrandt Peale, son of Marylander and artist Charles Wilson Peale. Completed in 1814 and designed by Robert Carey Long Sr., the Peale is thought to be the first building in America built specifically as an art museum. Ironically, it was used, instead, as a city hall, a school, as office space, and ultimately a factory. Happily, parts of the building have been returned to their intended use, displaying works by the elder Peale and other local artists (410-396-1149).

On leaving the Peale turn left and walk to the next corner, Lexington Street. Turn left onto Lexington and the **Zion Church (5),** completed in 1807, will be on the left. The congregation was established in 1755 by German Lutherans. Need to rest a bit? The church has a small garden facing Holliday Street.

At the next corner turn right onto Gay Street and see the **War Memorial (6)** on the left, dedicated in 1925 to Marylanders killed in World War I.

Option A: Port Discovery, the Kid-Powered Museum, is close by. The museum is the joint effort of the Rouse Company and Walt Disney Imagineering. Hands-on exhibits cover three floors in this former 19th-century fish market. To reach the museum, turn left from Gay Street onto Water Street. The museum will be on the left at 35 Market Place (410-727-8120, www.portdiscovery.org).

Walk down Gay Street. Just beyond Water Street, the **U.S. Customs House (7),** designed by Hornblower and Marshall and completed in 1907, will be on the right. Step inside and admire the four-story central atrium, stenciled walls, and ornamental molded plaster. The Call Room ceiling is painted with a vast mural, *Entering Port,* that measures 30 feet by 65 feet. On leaving the Customs House note the Holocaust Memorial, dedicated in 1997, across the street.

From Gay Street turn left onto Lombard Street and walk to the **Carroll Mansion (8),** which will be on the left at the corner of Front Street. Built in 1808, the red-brick, three-story Federal town house was acquired by Charles Carroll, a signer of the Declaration of Independence, who made it his in-town winter home. He died here in 1832 (410-752-1624, www.1840splaza.com).

Walk up North Front Street and stop at number 9, another Federal-style town house. The **Thorowgood Smith House (9)** was built in 1794 and later became the home of Smith, who was Baltimore's mayor from 1802 to 1804. The house is now owned and maintained by the Women's Civic League, who graciously welcome visitors. It is advisable to call before visiting (410-837-5424).

The massive, 215-foot-high column before you is the **Shot Tower (10).** What is a shot tower? Ammunition (lead pellets) were made in towers such as this one in the early 19th century. Molten lead was poured through a sieve. The lead dropped down the inside of the tower into water, forming round lead pellets or shot. While there were many shot towers, this is one of the few still standing. Its cornerstone was laid by neighbor Charles Carroll in 1828. Over one million bricks were used to build the tower. Its wall, $4^1/2$ feet thick at the base, taper to 1 foot, 9 inches at the top.

From the shot tower you may see the spire of St. Vincent de Paul Roman Catholic Church (1841) to the northwest. Interestingly, the church's architect was also its founder and first pastor: the Reverend John B. Gildea.

Option B: To visit the Jewish Museum of Maryland, with your back to Shot Tower Park turn left onto Baltimore Street, cross Exeter Street, and then turn right onto Lloyd Street. The Lloyd Street Synagogue will be on the left. A Greek Revival design by Robert Cary Long Jr., it was built in 1845. It is Baltimore's oldest synagogue, and the third-oldest synagogue in America. A few steps farther down Lloyd Street is the B'nai Israel Synagogue (1876), the oldest synagogue in Baltimore in continuous use. Both historic sites are linked by the Jewish Museum of Maryland. The museum offers exhibits, lectures, performances, and other programs, as well as a library and gift shop (410-732-6400, www.jewishmuseummd.org). When you leave the museum, to return to the main tour turn left, and you will be at the end of Lloyd Street. Turn right onto Lombard Street and walk 2 blocks to the corner of Albemarle Street. Rejoin the main tour at the 1840 House.

With your back to Shot Tower Park, cross Baltimore Street and walk down Lombard Street, stopping at the 1840 House at 50 Albemarle Street. A restored working-class dwelling, the house is open for tours (410-752-1624, www.1840splaza.com).

On leaving the 1840 House turn right, cross Lombard Street, walk down Albemarle Street, and turn right onto Pratt Street. The **Star-Spangled Banner Flag**

House (11) will be on the right at 844 East Pratt Street. This was the home of Mary Pickersgill, who hand-sewed the 30-by-42-foot flag that flew over Fort McHenry on September 14, 1814. It was the sight of that flag under bombardment by the British that inspired Francis Scott Key to write "The Star-Spangled Banner." The house, furnished with Federal-period pieces, is open for tours. Visit the 1812 Museum and its garden shaded by magnolia trees. The garden has a map of the United States that contains a stone from each state. There is also a museum store in which flags and other items are sold (410-837-1794, www.flaghouse.org/).

On leaving the house turn right onto Pratt Street and then left onto Fallsway Street, which becomes President Street. From President Street turn right onto Eastern Avenue. The **Baltimore Public Works Museum (12)** will be on the left at number 751. Housed in a former pumping station built about 1911, the museum offers an interactive, hands-on approach to learning the fascinating technology behind tunnels, roads, bridges, clean water, wastewater, and recycling (410-396-5565).

Return to President Street and turn right. The **Baltimore Civil War Museum (13)** will be on the right at number 601. Operated by the Maryland Historical Society, it occupies the President Street Station (1851). Frederick Douglass escaped to freedom at this rail station. The museum has exhibits about Douglass' escape, the station, railroad history, and many aspects of the Civil War (410-385-5188, www.mdhs.org).

Your self-guided walking tour ends here. Little Italy, to the east of the Baltimore Civil War Museum, has many restaurants, grocery stores, and markets. Turn left from the door of the museum onto President Street, then right onto Eastern Avenue, and then left onto Albemarle, High, or Exeter Streets. Alternately, you may walk west along the Inner Harbor, exploring its shops and eateries (see "Baltimore: The Inner Harbor").

26 • Annapolis: The Capitol and the City

Directions: *By car:* From the Capital Beltway take US 50 east. Take exit 24 to Rowe Boulevard south. *By public transportation:* Greyhound/Trailways has service between Washington and Annapolis (1-800-231-2222, www.greyhound.com).

Annapolis is named for Queen Anne, who gave the city its charter in 1708. Prior to that the town, founded by Puritans in 1649, had several names: Providence, Proctor's Town, the Town at the Severn, and Anne Arundel Town. In 1694 Maryland's capital was moved here from St. Mary's City.

Begin your tour at **Church Circle (1).** The church circled is St. Anne's Episcopal. The parish dates to 1692. Two earlier churches stood on this site, the first one built in 1706 and the second in 1796. When the second church burned in 1858 its walls and tower remained, forming the core for the present building. The parish has a silver communion service, which was given by King William III in 1696. Step inside. The St. Anne's Memorial Window was made by Tiffany and Company and was awarded first prize when it was displayed at Chicago's World Columbia Exposition in 1893.

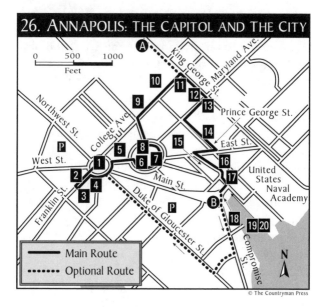

26. ANNAPOLIS: THE CAPITOL AND THE CITY

— Main Route

••••• Optional Route

© The Countryman Press

After seeing the church, walk counterclockwise around Church Circle, starting at the post office at the corner of Northwest Street. West Street will be next, where the visitors center is tucked away a few steps from Church Circle at 26 West Street.

Reynold's Tavern (2) is at 7 Church Circle between West and Franklin Streets. Built for William Reynolds in 1755, it was later used as a bank and then as a library. It is now owned by the National Trust for Historic Preservation.

Walk down Franklin Street. On the left at number 84 you'll see the **Banneker-Douglass Museum (3),** which is housed in the city's oldest African Methodist Episcopal Church, founded in 1803 and built in 1897. The museum presents exhibits, films, lectures, and other programs regarding African American history (410-216-6180).

Return to Church Circle. On the right, between Franklin and South Streets, is the **Anne Arundel County Circuit Courthouse (4).** Built in 1824, the courthouse was enlarged in 1892 and again in 1994.

Resume your walk around Church Circle. The Maryland Inn is tucked between Duke of Gloucester and Main Streets. Built in colonial times, it has always been an operating inn. Note the original Flemish bond brickwork and stone foundations. The mansard roof and Second Empire details were added in 1869.

Walk just a bit farther and leave Church Circle by turning right onto School Street. On the left will be **Government House (5),** the governor's official residence. Built in the Second Empire style in 1870, the mansion was remodeled as a five-part Georgian Manor in 1936; further renovations were done in 1987. Decorated with Maryland antiques, Government House is open to the public for tours by appointment (410-974-3531, www.gov.state.md.us).

You are now at State Circle. Note the John Shaw House to the right, at number 21 State Circle. Built in the 1720s, this is now used as state office space and is not open to the public. John Shaw was a very well-known cabinetmaker whose furniture you will see later on this tour in the statehouse and museums.

Cross the street to the **State House (6).** The first capitol was erected on this site in 1698, and the second in 1707. The cornerstone for the present capitol was laid in 1772. It took seven years to complete the building. Look at the dome. Designed by Joseph Clark, it is the nation's largest wooden dome built without nails.

Walk clockwise and enter the statehouse near North Street. The Old Senate Chamber will be on your right, furnished with some John Shaw pieces. The United States Congress met in this room from November 1783 to June 1784 and this is where Congress ratified the Treaty of Paris, ending the American Revolution. Also, on December 23, 1783, George Washington resigned his position as commander-in-chief of the Continental Army in this chamber.

Walk around the first floor of the capitol and view the historic exhibit. A major extension was added to the statehouse in 1906, and the legislature now meets in more spacious chambers. Interestingly, the Maryland Statehouse is the oldest state capitol in continuous legislative use (410-974-3400, www.gov.state.md.us).

Before you leave State Circle and the capitol grounds there are two more sites worth visiting. The **Old Treasury Building (7),** opposite the foot of East Street, was built in 1735 and is Maryland's oldest public building. Restored in 1949, the Historic Annapolis Foundation opens it to visitors by appointment (410-267-7619, www.annapolis.org). Also note the **statue of Thurgood Marshall (8).** Marshall (1908–1993) was a Marylander and the first African American Supreme Court justice. His memorial, modeled by Toby Mendez, was dedicated in 1996.

Leave State Circle at North Street. Walk to the end of North Street and then turn right onto College Avenue. **St. John's College (9)** will be on the left. King William's School was founded in 1696, and in 1784 it was succeeded by St. John's College. A famous alumnus was Francis Scott Key, who penned "The Star-Spangled Banner." Visit **McDowell Hall (10).** When the

ROBERT J. REGALBUTO

Government House and the Capitol

construction began in 1742 the hall was planned to be Governor Thomas Bladen's mansion. Left unfinished due to lack of legislative funding, it was labeled Bladen's Folly. When St. John's opened in 1784, it housed the entire college: classrooms, dining hall, and living quarters. It is named for the college's first president (410-263-2371, www.sjca.edu).

Option A: Two more buildings on the college campus are worth noting. The Barrister House, on King George Street, was built for Dr. Charles Carroll in 1724. Rescued from the wrecker's ball by the Historic Annapolis Foundation, it is now used as office space by the college. The other building is the Mitchell Gallery, where changing exhibits are mounted.

Leave St. John's on College Street. Turn left and stop at King George Street. **Ogle Hall (11)** will be on the right corner. Built in 1739, it was later lived in by the Ogle family. Samuel Ogle was the governor of Maryland and in 1775 his son Benjamin added the ballroom to the house. Both George Washington and the Marquis de

Lafayette were entertained here. Since 1944 Ogle Hall has been the Naval Academy's Alumni House (410-263-6933, www.usna.edu).

Turn right onto King George Street and right onto Maryland Avenue. The **Chase-Lloyd House (12)** will be on the right at number 22. This property was once owned by Edward Lloyd IV of Maryland's Eastern Shore and later acquired by Samuel Chase. Chase, a signer of the Declaration of Independence, built this house (1769–74), and in 1802 his daughter Mary married Francis Scott Key within its walls. The house is open for tours (410-263-2723).

Opposite the Chase-Lloyd house stands the **Harmon Harwood House (13).** Built in 1774, it was the last house designed by architect William Buckland. Note the finely carved entrance. Furnished with 18th-century Maryland furniture and artwork, the house is open to visitors. Be sure to visit the lovely gardens, too (410-263-4683, www.annapolis.net/harmonharwood/).

Walk along Maryland Avenue 1 block to Prince George Street. Turn left, and the **William Paca House and Garden (14)** will be on the left. Roberto Paca left Italy, lived in England for a time, and ultimately settled in Maryland in 1657. His descendant William Paca (1740–1799) was a three-term Maryland governor and a signer of the Declaration of Independence. He built this five-part Georgian mansion in 1763. Restored and furnished with period pieces and fine artwork, the house and its 2 acres of well-manicured gardens are open to the public by the Historic Annapolis Foundation. If you visit one historic house in Annapolis, this should be it (410-267-7619, www.annapolis.org).

On leaving the Paca House continue down Prince

George Street to the next corner. Turn right onto East Street then take a sharp left onto Pinkney Street. On the right at number 43 you'll see the **Barracks (16).** An early 18th-century building, this was used as military housing during the American Revolution. It is another Historic Annapolis Foundation property and is open by appointment (410-267-7619, www.annapolis.org).

Farther along Pinkney Street you'll see the **Shiplap House (17)** on the left at number 18. One of the oldest buildings in Annapolis, it was built circa 1715 and was used as a tavern. It is open to the public by the Historic Annapolis Foundation (410-267-7619, www.anna-polis.org). Farther along, at 4 Pinkney street, the early 19th-century Waterfront Warehouse will be on your left.

Continue walking until you arrive at Market Space. On the left, at the corner of Randall Street, is Middle-ton Tavern. Walk across the street to the **Market House (18).** There has been a market on this site since the 1780s. The present Market House was built in 1858 and restored in 1970 through the efforts of the Historic Annapolis Foundation.

Cross Randall Street to **Dock Square (19).** Note the **Kunta Kinte–Alex Haley Memorial (20).** Alex Haley (1921–92), the author of *Roots*, is depicted reading a book to a group of children of various ethnic back-grounds. He gestures toward the Chesapeake Bay, telling the story of the arrival of his ancestor Kunta Kinte and his companions. The sculpture group, modeled by Ed Dwight, was dedicated in 1999. A nearby plaque com-memorates the arrival of Kunta Kinte in the port of Annapolis (www.kintehaley.org/memorial).

Your tour ends here. Explore the shops and restau-rants in Dock Square and along Main Street, which will

Kunta Kinte–Alex Haley Memorial

lead you back to Church Circle where this tour began.

Should you wish to take this book's tour of the Naval Academy (see the next chapter), the Academy's Gate 1, the tour's start, is just 2 blocks from city dock. With your back to the harbor, turn right on Randall Street and walk to Gate 1.

Option B: You may also return to Church Circle by way of Duke of Gloucester Street, with more historic sites along the way. Facing the harbor veer to the right on Compromise Street. Then turn left onto St. Mary's Street. St. Mary's ends at Duke of Gloucester Street. The Charles Carroll House will be in front of you at number 107. This is birthplace and home of Charles Carroll, the only Roman Catholic to sign the Declaration of Independence. The house dates to 1680, and additions were made during the two centuries following (410-269-1737). St. Mary's Roman Catholic Church next door is a Victorian Gothic Revival design, built in 1860.

From St. Mary's turn left on Duke of Gloucester Street. On the opposite side of the street, numbers

110–114, is Ridout Row and, just beyond that, the Ridout House at number 120. The house was built for Englishman John Ridout in 1764; the adjoining row houses were built for tenants in 1774.

City Hall will be next on the right. The 18th-century Assembly Rooms, which stood on this site, were destroyed by fire during the Civil War and replaced with the present building.

Walk to Conduit Street. The First Presbyterian Church (410-267-8705) will be on the left. Founded in 1846, the church occupies the Old Hallam Theatre, which was built in 1826. Number 138 Conduit Street was the home of Charles Zimmerman, who composed "Anchors a'Weigh," the navy's anthem.

Cross the Duke of Gloucester Street to 164 Conduit Street. William Pickney was born in this house in 1764. Pickney was a congressman, senator, U.S. attorney general, and ambassador to Great Britain, Russia, and the Kingdom of Naples. The house was moved to this site in 1972 and is now a private residence.

Return to Duke of Gloucester Street and walk to Church Circle, where the main tour began.

27 · Annapolis: The U.S. Naval Academy

Directions: *By car:* From the Capital Beltway take US 50 east. Take exit 27 and follow the signs to the U.S. Naval Academy. Once over the Naval Academy Bridge turn right at the second light to Gate 1. *By public transportation:* Greyhound/Trailways has bus service to Washington and Annapolis (1-800-231-2222, www.greyhound.com).

George Bancroft, secretary of the Navy, founded the U.S. Naval Academy in 1845. After the Battle of Bull Run, Abraham Lincoln agreed to have the academy moved to Newport, Rhode Island, as a precautionary measure. In 1865 the academy returned to Annapolis. Many of the beaux arts buildings on the 300-acre campus were designed by Ernest Flagg at the turn of the last century. In 1976 women were first admitted to the Naval Academy, where students are known as midshipmen. Why midshipmen? On 19th-century ships officers were berthed aft and the crew in the bow. Officers-in-training were berthed between them, or midship, and so they became known as midshipmen. Today the Naval Academy enrolls about 4,000 midshipmen.

Enter the academy through **Gate 1 (1),** near the

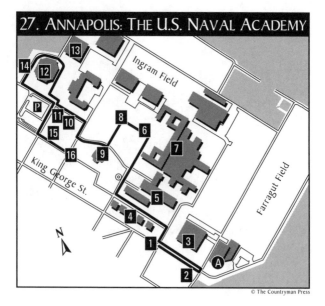

27. ANNAPOLIS: THE U.S. NAVAL ACADEMY

© The Countryman Press

intersection of King George Street and Randall Street. Be prepared to undergo a security check; you must have a photo ID. Backpacks are not allowed though the gate. For an update on security procedures, contact the academy before your visit (410-263-6933, www.usna.edu).

Proceed straight ahead to the **Armel-Leftwich Visitor Center (2),** which features the orientation film *To Lead and To Serve* and interactive exhibits. There is also a gift shop.

Option A: The Naval Academy Athletic Association's (NAAA) ticket office is at Ricketts Hall, which is to the right as you leave the visitors center.

Retrace your steps, returning to Gate 1. **LeJeune Hall (3)** will be on the right. This is the academy's physical education center. Enter and go to the second floor to visit the Athletic Hall of Fame and to see the Olympic-sized swimming pool and the wrestling arena.

In front to LeJeune Hall, at the corner of Cooper Road, you will see the navy's mascot, Bill the Goat. From Cooper Road turn left and walk along Porter Road. **Officers' housing (4)** is on the left. On the right, at the far side of the tennis courts, is **Dahlgren Hall (5).** Open to visitors, Dahlgren Hall includes dining facilities.

At the first corner turn right and walk toward the **statue of Tecumseh (6),** a bronze replica of the USS *Delaware*'s wooden figurehead of the Indian warrior. To the right is **Bancroft Hall (7),** a huge dormitory named after the academy's founder and known to the midshipmen as Mother B. The meal formations for the brigade of midshipmen occur in front of Mother B at 12:05 PM weekdays in spring and fall.

With your back to Bancroft Hall walk across the Yard on Stribling Walk. In the center, at the **Mexican Monument (8),** turn left and walk toward the chapel. The obelisk on the right is a monument to Naval Officer W.L. Herndon. The gazebo on the left is used for concerts.

The **Chapel (9),** or Cathedral of the Navy, was designed by Flagg and dedicated in 1908. Step inside. The stained-glass windows commemorating naval heroes were made by Tiffany and by Gorham Studios. Protestant services and Roman Catholic masses are regularly scheduled. Poignantly, a pew is always left empty as a reminder of prisoners of war and those missing in action.

Descend to the chapel's crypt, the resting place of John Paul Jones. A Scotsman, Jones was a hero during the American Revolution whose most famous words

Midshipmen in front of Bancroft Hall

were "I have not yet begun to fight." Jones died in Paris in 1792. In 1905 his remains were brought here, and they now lie in a marble and bronze sarcophagus.

On leaving the chapel turn left and walk to **Preble Hall (10)** on the right, home of the U.S. Naval Academy Museum. This is an outstanding collection of more than 35,000 objects, including paintings and other artwork and artifacts. Adjacent to the museum is the Class of 1951 Gallery of Ships, one of the finest collections of ship models in the world. Some models are made of gold; others are made of bone or wood.

When you leave Preble Hall turn left and walk down Decatur Road. On the left is the **Tripoli Monument (11)** and beyond that Leahy Hall, which houses the admissions office. Just beyond Leahy Hall the immense building on your right is **Alumni Hall (12).** It can seat over 5,700 people; athletic events, concerts, plays, and lectures take place here. Turn right at Alumni Hall. The **Nimitz Library (13)** is in front of you. If you circle Alumni Hall you will see the **Vietnam Memorial (14),** which overlooks Dorsey Creek and the rest of the campus on the opposite shore. A footbridge spans the creek.

Facing the creek turn left, and Worden Field (the Parade Grounds) will be in front of you. Turn left onto Decatur Avenue, right onto College Avenue, and left onto Hanover Street. The **Officers and Faculty Club (15)** will be on the left. The club is open to the public for lunch on weekdays.

A few steps farther down Hanover Street is **Gate 3 (16),** where you may exit the academy grounds, or you may exit at Gate 1 where this walking tour began.

28 · Easton

Directions: *By car:* From the Capital Beltway take US 50 east directly to Easton. Follow the signs to downtown on Dover Street and turn left onto Washington Street and park at the Historical Society. *By public transportation:* Greyhound has bus service to Easton (1-800-231-2222, www.greyhound.com).

English settlers began establishing tobacco plantations here on the Chesapeake Bay's Eastern Shore as early as the 1650s. In 1661 this became Maryland's Talbot County, named in honor of Lord Baltimore's sister, Lady Grace Talbot. Quakers founded the county seat in 1682. At first known as Talbot Court House, in 1789 the name was changed to Easton, since this was the "East Town" and Maryland's eastern-shore capital.

Begin your walking tour at the **Historical Society of Talbot County (1),** at 25 South Washington Street between Dover Street and Glenwood Avenue. Its museum has a collection of 40,000 artifacts that document the county's history from precolonial times to the present. In addition to the museum the historical society has three houses on-site that are open to visitors: a 17th-century house known as Ending of Controversie, the 18th-century Joseph Neall House, and the 19th-century James Neall house. Other facilities include a

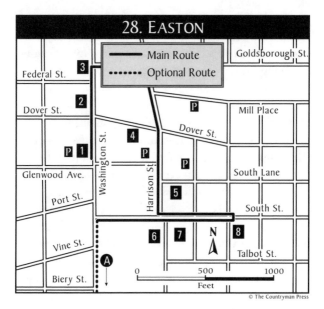

© The Countryman Press

research library, archives, a consignment shop, and a museum store. All are set within an award-winning Federal-style garden (410-822-0773, www.hstc.org).

When you leave the historical society turn left onto Washington Street. Note the High Victorian Gothic Revival Odd Fellows Lodge (1879) on the left at the corner of Dever Street. Ahead of you on the left is **Courthouse Square (2).** The first courthouse was built on this spot in 1710 and replaced by the present building in 1794. Over the years additions have been made (410-770-8001).

Just ahead on your left, beyond Federal Street, you'll see the **Old Brick Hotel (3),** built circa 1811. Both the County Courthouse and the Old Brick Hotel were visited by Frederick Douglass in 1878. Douglass was born a slave in this county in 1818, escaped to freedom in 1838, and became a leading abolitionist. In 1878 he returned to Easton at the invitation of the Talbot County Republicans. He stayed as a guest at the Brick Hotel, despite the fact that it was segregated, and gave a speech at the Court House.

Continue to walk on Washington Street. Turn right onto Goldsborough Street and then right again onto Harrison Street. Walk to Dover Street and look to the right at the **Avalon Theater (4).** Built as a movie theater in 1921, the Avalon was restored to its art deco splendor, and its facilities were completely updated with state-of-the-art lighting and sound. A true showplace, the Avalon is now the Eastern Shore's performing arts center. In addition to the auditorium, the upper floor of the Avalon is crowned with a stained glass dome and offers a panoramic view of town (410-822-0345, www.avalontheater.com).

Resume your walk along Harrison Street. The **Inn at Easton (5),** built about 1794, will be on the left at the corner of South Lane. Pass the Armory on the left and cross South Street. On the right is **Christ Church (6).** Members of the Church of England founded the parish in 1692. This granite structure is the congregation's fifth church building. A William Strickland design, it was under construction from 1840 to 1845 and has been enlarged and modified since. The rectory is to the right of the church. Dating to 1856, the rectory was designed by Richard Upjohn, whose best-known work is Trinity Church in New York City (410-822-2677).

Across from Christ Church is the **Academy of Fine Arts (7).** Here a farmhouse and a school built in 1820 have been adapted for use as an art museum and cul-

ROBERT J. REGALBUTO

The Courthouse

tural center. The academy has a light-filled atrium, five galleries, a library, studios, conference rooms, and a sculpture garden. A wide variety of programs and exhibits, concerts, school programs, trips, and classes make the academy a lively and stimulating arts center (410-822-0455, www.art-academy.org).

Walk down South Street past the Gothic Revival cottages on the right which were built about 1875. Turn right onto Hanson Street. The redbrick **Bethel African Methodist Episcopal Church (8)** will be on the left. During his 1878 visit to Easton, Frederick Douglass spoke to a large gathering of former slaves here.

Retrace your steps along South Street, past the Academy and Christ Church, until you reach Washington Street. Turn right onto Washington Street and return to the starting point of this tour.

Option A: It is a half-mile walk from the corner of Washington and South Streets to the Third Haven Meeting House, at 405 South Washington. Built in 1684, this

Quaker meeting house is the oldest religious building in America still in use and it is the oldest building in Maryland. The meetinghouse was widened in 1797; the front porch was added later. George Fox, the founder of the Society of Friends, donated the first books to the meetinghouse's library, and it is known that another famous Quaker, William Penn, visited here. If planning a visit, call in advance (410-822-0293).

29 · St. Michaels

Directions: *By car:* From the Capital Beltway take US 50 east to Maryland's Eastern Shore. Then take MD 322 to MD 33 west to St. Michaels. *By public transportation:* There is no public transportation to St. Michaels. However, Greyhound/Trailways (1-800-231-2222, www.greyhound.com) has service to Easton. It is an 11-mile cab ride to St. Michaels (Bay Country Taxi, 410-770-9030).

The picturesque village of St. Michaels, nestled between Broad Creek and the Mile River, was founded in 1778 by James Braddock. The relatively young town was attacked by the British during the War of 1812. On August 10, 1813, as St. Michaels was being bombarded on a foggy night, townsfolk extinguished all their lights and hung lanterns high on the tops of trees so that the British aim would be too high. The trick worked. The town was spared heavy damage and St. Michaels has since been known as "the town that fooled the British." Once a boatbuilding center, the community later turned to oystering and today is a popular resort town with many yachts in its harbor.

Your walk begins at the **corner** of the town's main street, North Talbot, and Cherry Streets **(1).** Walk down Cherry Street and stop at number 203, on the left, **the**

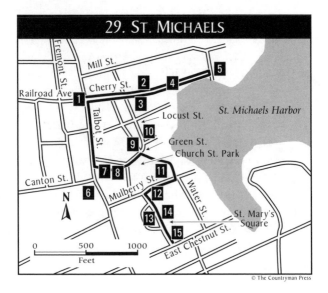

29. ST. MICHAELS

© The Countryman Press

Snuggery (2). This house was built in the late 1700s. The siding you see today hides its original, 18-inch-thick log construction. The house opposite the Snuggery, at 200 Cherry, was built as a tavern in 1799, later used as a residence and enlarged, and today is the **Dr. Dodson House Bed & Breakfast (3).** In 1877, Frederick Douglass was a visitor to this house—then owned by Louisa, the daughter of Thomas Auld. Auld had been one of Douglass' masters, and the two men, former master and slave, met here as friends.

Continue walking along Cherry Street and cross the **footbridge (4),** the most recent of a series of bridges that have spanned this spot over the last two centuries. The bridge leads to the **Chesapeake Bay Maritime**

Museum (5). Occupying an expansive site along the waterfront, the museum features nine buildings, including a restored 1879 lighthouse and the world's largest collection of traditional Chesapeake Bay boats, including a skipjack used for harvesting oysters and a log-bottom bogeye. Permanent exhibits feature nautical history and decoy displays. At the museum's Waterman's Wharf you may try your hand at harvesting oysters and crabs (410-745-2916, www.cbmm.org).

Retrace your steps on Cherry Street to the starting point of the tour. Turn left onto North Talbot Street. Note the white cupola ahead of you on the right that crowns the redbrick, Italianate **St. Luke's United Methodist Church (6),** built in 1871.

Enter the churchyard of **Christ Church (7),** on the left. This Anglican-Episcopal congregation was founded in 1672, which makes it older than the town itself. This is the third church to stand on this spot. The first was a clapboard building (1709), the second a redbrick church (1814). This brick and granite building, reminiscent of English Gothic country churches, was built in 1878 and restored a century later. The church displays gifts given it by Queen Anne at the beginning of the 18th century, including the silver communion service in the display case and the baptismal font under the pulpit. Walk through the churchyard to the rear of the church. The oldest graves date to 1672. Exit through the **lynch gate (8).** Commonplace in medieval English churchyards, lynch gates were the entryway to the graveyard for a lynch, or corpse.

After exiting through the lynch gate turn left and then right onto Green Street. Locust Street will be on the left, flanked by two colonial houses: the **Bruff-Mansfield**

Chesapeake Bay Maritime Museum

House (9), built in 1778, on the left and the **Thomas Harrison House (10),** circa 1798, on the right.

Enter Church Creek Park and follow the path diagonally to the left. Note the two cannons on the waterfront. Dedicated in 1975, these are replicas of cannons used here in 1813.

Walk through the lot to Mulberry Street. The house on your right is the **birthplace of Amelia Welby (11),** once Maryland's poet laureate. The house was built at the close of the 18th century.

Walk a few steps along Mulberry Street to the next corner on the left and a dwelling known as **the Cannon Ball House (12).** In 1813, during the Battle of St. Michaels, a British cannonball flew through this house's roof and then bounced down its staircase, step by step!

Turn left at this corner and approach **St. Mary's Square (13),** the town's marketing center two centuries ago. The redbrick **Masonic Lodge (14)** on the left was built as a Methodist Church in 1839. It served as a school for a time before becoming a lodge. Across the way, in the square's center, note the small antique cannon and the bell.

St. Mary's Square Museum (15) is at the far end of the square. Occupying a house built in 1865, the museum permanently displays artifacts and furnishings that illustrate St. Michaels history (410-745-9561).

After visiting the museum walk on East Chestnut Street to Talbot Street, returning to the starting point of this walk.

30 · St. Mary's City

Directions: *By car:* From the Capital Beltway take MD 5 south to Historic St. Mary's City. *By public transportation:* There is no public transportation to St. Mary's City.

St. Mary's City was settled by the English in 1634. Led by the Roman Catholic Calvert family (the Lords of Baltimore), Maryland was envisioned as a refuge where Catholics could worship openly. St. Mary's City was the colony's first capital. In the 17th century the impressive redbrick capitol was surrounded by homes, law offices, inns, and ordinaries (eating places). There was also a redbrick chapel. When Maryland's capital was moved to Annapolis in 1695, the 60-year-old St. Mary's City declined in importance, its buildings abandoned and left to decay. In 1934 St. Mary's 300th anniversary was commemorated, which sparked a renewed interest in the settlement. In 1966 Maryland established the Historic St. Mary's City Commission. Excavations are ongoing, unearthing long-lost artifacts. The Old State House and some other buildings have been rebuilt, some in their entirety, others as ghost structures where post and beam give an indication of where a house stood, and your imagination does the rest. In the near future the redbrick, barrel-vaulted chapel will be reconstructed on its original site. The historic area covers a

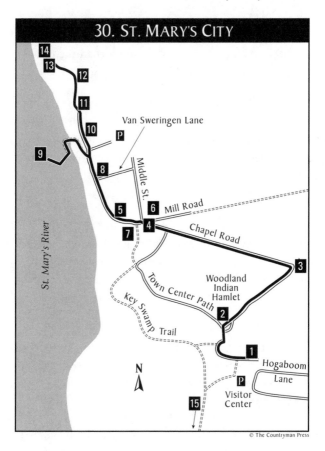

30. ST. MARY'S CITY

Van Sweringen Lane

Middle St.

Mill Road

Chapel Road

St. Mary's River

Town Center Path

Key Swamp Trail

Woodland Indian Hamlet

Hogaboom Lane

Visitor Center

N

© The Countryman Press

campus of 850 acres, which includes natural areas.

This self-guided walking tour will lead you through the areas restored by the Historic St. Mary's City Foundation, including a woodland Indian hamlet, the town center, the ship *The Maryland Dove*, and the Godiah Spray tobacco plantation. Consider taking the foundation's self-guided audio tour as well. Your visit will be enhanced by the informative wayside signs throughout the property. Historic St. Mary's City also presents living history, so be prepared to encounter costumed interpreters who will provided helpful, often entertaining, responses to your questions.

Begin at Historic St. Mary's City **visitors center (1).** An admission fee is charged (240-895-4990, 1-800-SMC-1634, www.hsma@smcm.edu). In winter the visitors center may be closed; enter the historic area through Farthing's Ordinary, about a half-mile north on MD 5.

Leave the visitors center and turn right to follow the path to the **Woodland Indian Hamlet (2).** When the English arrived the area was already inhabited. Leonard Calvert made peace with the Indians, and later on this walk you will see the monument that commemorates this. The hamlet includes a reconstructed longhouse, a *witchott.*

From the Indian hamlet take the path on the right, Chapel Field Path. St. Mary's first chapel was a room in the Jesuits' wooden house. In 1667 the Jesuits built a **brick chapel (3)** on this site. The cross-shaped building was 54 feet long and its crossing and transept spanned 57 feet. Closed by an act of the Maryland Assembly in 1704, the Jesuits demolished their chapel, preserving its bricks for subsequent buildings. Plans are underway to reconstruct the chapel on its original site.

Take the Chapel Road to the **Town Center (4).** At the intersection with Mill Road turn around and look back. Chapel Road veers to the right; Mill Road to the left. This is not by accident. A baroque plan was used to lay out St. Mary's City streets. Popular in 16th-century

St. Mary's City

Rome, the plan is essentially triangular. One corner is the town center, and the other points are for the chapel and the mill. Facing north, another triangle began at town center, with the jail at the northeast corner and the statehouse at the northwest.

Turn your attention to the site of the **Calvert House (5).** Built for Leonard Calvert, Maryland's first governor, it was later used as Maryland's first statehouse.

Cordea's Hope (6) is across Middle Road. Built by French immigrant Mark Cordea about 1675, it is believed that it was used as a storage facility.

Smith's Ordinary (7) is opposite Cordea's Hope. Built in 1666 by William Smith, it was destroyed by fire in 1678. Archaeological excavations in this, the town center, unearthed hundreds of artifacts in the 1980s and '90s.

Walk down Middle Street and turn left onto Van

Swearingen Lane. The site of **Van Swearingen's Inn (8)** will be on the right. In 1678, Garrett Van Swearingen, an enterprising man from Holland, bought a house built 14 years earlier and transformed it into St. Mary's City's best ordinary. It is also believed that this was America's first coffeehouse.

From the ghost structures of the inn turn right onto Aldermanbury Street, and the *Maryland Dove* (9) will be docked on the left. Two ships, the *Ark* and the *Dove*, brought 140 colonists to these shores in 1634. This replica of the *Dove* is a square-rigged ship that you may board and there listen to costumed sailors tell old yarns.

Return to Aldermanbury Road and resume your walk north. **Farthing's Ordinary (10)** will be on the right. Built in 1984, the ordinary houses Historic St. Mary's City museum shop. Walk a few more steps and you'll come across the 1934 reconstruction of the **Old State House (11),** which was originally built in 1676. Step inside to view the interior; costumed interpreters are on hand to answer your questions.

Continue your trek north to **Trinity Church (12).** This Episcopal church was built in 1829 with bricks salvaged from the 1676 statehouse. A few steps father on is the actual **1676 statehouse site (13).** The building was not reconstructed here in 1934 because of graves on the site. The **obelisk (14)** nearby marks the spot and commemorates Leonard Calvert's treaty with a Yaocamaco Indian chief.

Retrace your steps past the visitors center and walk to the **Godiah Spray Tobacco Plantation (15).** Today a working farm using 17th-century tools and implements, the plantation is populated with costumed interpreters and farm animals. Be sure to see the dwelling house, a freedman's cottage, tobacco-drying barns, animal pens, the kitchen garden, and the tobacco fields.

From the plantation you may continue to explore the property on the nature trail, completing your visit to 17th-century Maryland.

31 · Frederick

Directions: *By car:* From the Capital Beltway take I-270 north to MD 15 in Frederick. Take the West Patrick Street exit. Bear right onto West South Street and then turn left onto Market Street to downtown. *By public transportation:* Greyhound has bus service to Frederick (1-800-231-2222, www.greyhound.com). During the week there is commuter service: from the Washington Metro station at Shady Grove take the MTA bus #991 to Frederick, or a MARC commuter train (Brunswick Line). For commuter bus or train schedule information call 410-539-5000 or 866-RIDE-MTA.

Fredericktown, as the city was first named, was settled by German and English colonists in 1745. In his poem "Barbara Fritchie," John Greenleaf Whittier describes Frederick:

> *Up from the meadows thick with corn.*
> *Clear in the cool September morn,*
> *The clustered spires of Frederick stand*
> *Green-walled by the hills of Maryland.*

On this tour you will see many of the tall spires Whittier alludes to, as well as the home of Barbara Fritchie (Frietschie).

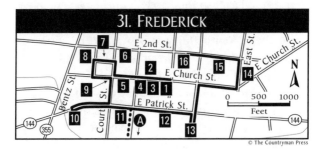

© The Countryman Press

Start at the **Historical Society of Frederick County (1),** at 24 East Church Street. Built as a home for a physician and his family in 1820, it later housed the Loats Female Orphan Asylum and, since 1959, it has been the historical society's museum. Tours are given of the house, which is filled with period furnishings, costumes, works by local artists and artisans, memorabilia, and an outstanding collection of tall-case clocks made right here in Frederick. There is also a research library, a book store, and a garden in which to rest a bit before beginning your walk (301-663-1188, www. fwp.net/hsfc).

When you leave the historical society look directly across Church Street to what are undoubtedly the most elegant twin spires in Frederick. German settlers founded the **Evangelical Lutheran Church (2)** in 1738. The present church, built in 1858, is the congregation's third, and incorporates parts of the stone church built in 1762.

Turn left and on the left, at 21 East Church Street, is **Winchester Hall (3).** The Greek Revival hall was built in 1843 as the Frederick Female Seminary, served as a Union hospital during the Civil War, and was the nucleus for Hood College until 1930. Winchester Hall today houses the county offices.

Redbrick **Kemp Hall (4)** is next, at the corner of Market Street. Built in 1860, it played a pivotal role in Maryland's history the following year. On the eve of the Civil War, Annapolis (the state capital) was in the hands of Federal troops and the state legislature decided to meet at Kemp Hall to debate whether or not Maryland should secede from the Union. No decision was made; ultimately Maryland remained in the Union.

Continue along Church street, crossing Market Street. **Trinity Chapel (5)** will be on the left. Its German Reformed congregation founded in 1746, the stone church you see was built in 1763. When the congregation outgrew Trinity Chapel it built the Greek Revival Evangelical Reformed Church just across the street in 1848. A unique design, the church does not have twin spires, but rather twin cupolas. This was the church Barbara Fritchie attended. Today both chapel and church are in the United Church of Christ.

Turn right onto Court Street and stop at number 104 North Court. This diminutive building once housed the **law offices (6)** of two prominent Americans: Francis Scott Key (author of "The Star-Spangled Banner") and his brother-in-law Roger Brook Taney. Taney, in his role as chief justice of the Supreme Court, administered the oath of office to Abraham Lincoln.

Opposite the offices you'll see Council Street. Walk down **Council Street (7),** noting the twin Federal town houses on your right, both of which were built in 1815. Robert E. Lee stayed in number 103; the Marquis de Lafayette and, some years later, Andrew Jackson, were guests at number 105.

Turn left onto Record Street and the **Ramsey House (8)** will be on the right at number 119. Abraham Lincoln visited General George Hartstuff in this house in 1862 after the general had been wounded in the Battle of Antietam.

Turn left onto West Church Street. You are now in **Court Square (9)**; city hall is on the left. It was built as a courthouse in 1862. All Saints Episcopal Church is on the right. Founded in 1742, All Saints was designed in 1856 by Richard Upjohn, America's leading Early Gothic Revival architect, who also designed Trinity Church in New York City. All Saints was used as a hospital during the Civil War. The church interior is lit by stained-glass windows that reflect four different styles and periods.

From All Saints turn right onto Court Street. Walk past All Saints Parish Hall (an earlier church built in 1813) and then turn right onto West Patrick Street. Stop at the **Barbara Fritchie House (10)** at number 154. Barbara Fritchie (or Frietschie) was born Barbara Haver in Lancaster, Pennsylvania, in 1766. She married a glovemaker in 1806 and they settled in Frederick. Legend has it that on September 6, 1862, the defiant 95-year-old widow brazenly display the United States flag as Stonewall Jackson and his Confederates marched past her house. The Massachusetts Quaker and abolitionist John Greenleaf Whittier immortalized her in his poem "Barbara Fritchie." With some poetic license, Whittier wrote:

> *Up rose old Barbara Frietchie then,*
> *Bowed with her fourscore years and ten;*
> *Bravest of all in Frederick town,*
> *She took up the flag the men hauled down;*

In her attic window the staff she set,
  To show that one heart was loyal yet.
Up the street came the rebel tread,
  Stonewall Jackson riding ahead.
Under his slouched hat left and right
  He glanced; the old flag met his sight.
Halt! the dust-blown ranks stood fast.
  Fire! out blazed the rival-blast.
It shivered the window, pane and sash;
  It rent the banner with seam and gash.
Quick, as it fell, from the broken staff
  Dame Barbara snatched the silken scarf.
She leaned far out on the window-sill,
  and shook it forth with a royal will.
Shoot, if you must, this old gray head,
  But spare your country's flag, she said. . . .

The widow Fritchie died later that year. Her house, ruined in a flood six years later, was demolished. In 1926 the house was rebuilt as a museum. A legend in her own time, her cherished belongings were carefully preserved by her family and are on display: gloves made by her husband; quilts, linens, and doll clothing she made; her furniture, and other possessions (301-698-0630).

Reverse your direction on West Patrick Street and walk to Market Street. En route you will pass the art deco **Tivoli Theatre (11)** on the right. The Tivoli was built as a movie theater in 1926 and is now the Weinberg Center for the Arts.

Option A: It is a half-mile detour south on Market Street to Mount Olivet Cemetery, at number 515 South Market, where Barbara Fritchie is buried along with more than 800 Civil War soldiers, both Union and Con-

COURTESY OF THE TOURISM COUNCIL OF FREDERICK, MD

The clustered spires of Frederick

federate. On your way to the cemetery you'll see the old Baltimore and Ohio Railroad station on the left. Abraham Lincoln made a speech at this station following the Battle at Antietam. Also en route you'll see the Hessian Barracks (1777). Now on the grounds of the Maryland School for the Deaf, the barracks may be seen through the gates at 101 Clark Place (301-663-8687).

Resume your walk east on Patrick Street. The **National Museum of Civil War Medicine (12)** will be on the right at 48 East Patrick Street. Covering almost 7,000 square feet, the museum's exhibits focus on medical schools at the time of the Civil War, recruiting and enlisting, camp life, the evacuation of the wounded, dental care, and naval medicine, and include a field dressing station, a field hospital, an apothecary wagon, and a pavilion hospital (310-695-1864, www.civilwarmed.org).

Walk farther along East Patrick Street and turn right onto South Carroll Street. Walk a few steps down to

Carroll Creek and you will be delightfully surprised by the trompe l'oeil murals on this, the **Community Bridge (13),** the creation of artist William M. Cochran, with the help of 10 assistants. The artist's brush has transformed an ordinary concrete bridge into an ivy-covered stone bridge whose walls are punctuated with sculpture and portraiture. Begun in 1993, it was a 5-year project (301-698-2647, www.sharedvision.org). The Delaplaine Visual Arts Center is next to the bridge at 40 South Carroll Street.

After looking at the bridge reverse direction, walking up Carroll Street to East Church Street. Turn right onto East Church Street and walk around the block, turning left onto East Street past the modest 19th-century dwellings on **Shab Row (14)** and left onto East Second Street, noting the many Federal-style houses along the way.

The **Frederick Academy of the Visitation (15)** will be on the left at 200 East Second Street. The academy was a convent school founded by Mother Seton's Sisters of Charity in 1823. In 1846 the school changed hands when the Sisters of the Visitation arrived and built the present brick convent and school. Strictly cloistered, the Visitation nuns never left the convent to venture into Frederick. Visit the chapel, which is arguably Frederick's most beautiful.

Just one block away, beyond Chapel Alley, you'll see **St. John the Evangelist Roman Catholic Church (16).** The first Roman Catholic church was built in Frederick in 1763. The present Greek Revival church was built in 1834, and its spire is the tallest structure in the city. The church's interior is embellished with murals painted by Italian artists.

Turn left onto Maxwell Avenue, returning to the corner of East Church Street where this tour began.

Also Nearby

Schifferstadt Architectural Museum (301-663-3885)

Beatty-Cramer House (310-668-2086)

The Children's Museum of Rose Hill Manor (310-694-1648)

32 · Havre de Grace

Directions: *By car:* Take I-95 to exit 89. Take MD 155 east 4.5 miles to Havre de Grace. Once in town turn right onto Juanita Street, left onto Ostego Street, and right onto Union Avenue. The tour begins at the far end of Union. *By public transportation:* MTA has a commuter bus (#420) from Baltimore (410-539-5000, 1-866-RIDE-MTA, www.mtamaryland.com).

The Marquis de Lafayette is often credited with giving Havre de Grace its present name. In 1782, en route from Washington's Mount Vernon to Philadelphia, he traveled the Old Post Road, which passed through this town, then known as Susquehanna Lower Falls. Witnesses said that, on seeing the town and its waterways, Lafayette proclaimed *"C'est Le Havre,"* comparing this to the French port. The compliment was accepted and from that time onward the town has been Havre de Grace.

During the War of 1812 the town was bombarded and burned by the British. Later in the 19th century Havre de Grace rebuilt and rallied as a fishing port, and as a transportation and business center. Though the town declined in the 20th century, Havre de Grace is now enjoying a resurgence, as many people from Balti-

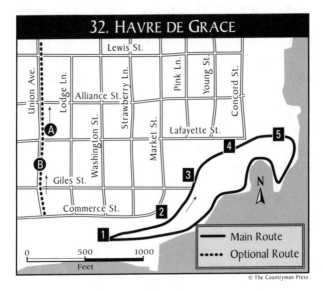

32. HAVRE DE GRACE

Lewis St.

Union Ave.
Lodge Ln.
Alliance St.
Strawberry Ln.
Washington St.
Market St.
Pink Ln.
Young St.
Lafayette St.
Concord St.

A
B
Giles St.
Commerce St.

1 **2** **3** **4** **5**

N

0   500   1000
Feet

—— Main Route
····· Optional Route

© The Countryman Press

more and beyond are discovering its history, charm, and placid waterways.

Begin at the foot of Union Avenue at **Tydings Memorial Park (1).** The park occupies a 17-acre site that for many years was known as Bayside Park. It was renamed in honor of favorite son Millard E. Tydings (1890–1961). As a U.S. senator, Tydings introduced the Philippines Independence Bill to Congress. The park overlooks a yacht basin, Chesapeake Bay, the Susquehanna Flats, and, in the distance, Tydings Island.

Note the fieldstone **Bayou Villa (2)** at 300 Commerce Street. Originally a luxury hotel, it was completed in 1920, closed during the Great Depression, became a convent, and more recently has been renovated and converted to condominiums.

Continue along Commerce Street to the **Havre de Grace Decoy Museum (3).** Founded in 1981, the museum has an impressive permanent collection of decoys and offers special programs and changing exhibits. Its library has the nation's most comprehensive collection of works on waterfowl species, the history of duck hunting, and the manufacture of decoys. The museum "exists to collect, document, preserve, and interpret waterfowl decoys as the art form applies to the heritage of Chesapeake Bay" (410-939-3739, www.decoymuseum.com).

From the Decoy Museum follow the brick path to the **Maritime Museum (4).** Focusing on Chesapeake Bay and the town's nautical history, the museum's permanent collection encompasses memorabilia, artifacts, and photos. The Susquehanna Flats Environmental Center and the Chesapeake Wooden Boat Builders School share the same facility (410-939-4800).

The brick path will next lead you to the **Concord Point Lighthouse (5).** A 36-foot-high granite tower, the walls of the lighthouse are more than 3 feet thick the base, tapering to 18 inches near the lantern. When the lighthouse opened in 1827 the lantern was lit by nine whale-oil lamps, each with a tin reflector. Concord Point Lighthouse was the oldest continuously operating lighthouse in Maryland when it was decommissioned in 1975. Both it and the lightkeepers house are being restored by the Maryland Historical Trust and both are open to visitors, who may enjoy the spectacular views of the Chesapeake Bay from the lantern room (410-939-9040).

After visiting the lighthouse walk along the boardwalk promenade for a half-mile stroll back to Tydings Memorial Park.

Option A: About 1½ miles north of Tydings Park is the Susquehanna Museum. Located at a lock of the Susquehanna and Tidewater Canal, a locktender's house (1840), office, and a pivot bridge have been restored. To reach the museum by foot, bicycle, or car go north on Union Avenue to the end of the street, bear left onto Water Street, and then turn right onto Consteo Street (410-939-5780).

Option B: Hutchins Park abuts the Susquehanna River. Docked there are two historic boats that offer cruises. The skipjack *Martha Lewis* (410-939-4078) is a V-bottomed, two-sail bateau that can accommodate 32 passengers. One of the last remaining oyster dredge boats, it cruises upper Chesapeake Bay. The other vessel is the *Lantern Queen* (410-287-7217), a century-old 97-foot-long paddlewheeler (410-287-7217). To reach Hutchins Park, head north on Union Avenue and turn right onto Congress Avenue. The distance between Tydings and Hutchins Parks is about 1¼ miles.

Also Nearby

Steppingstone Museum (410-939-2299, 1-888-419-1762, www.steppingstonemuseum.org)

IV. West Virginia

33 · Harpers Ferry

Directions: *By car:* From the Capital Beltway take I-270 north to US 340 west to Harpers Ferry. Follow the signs to the National Park Service visitor center. *By public transportation:* Both Amtrak (1-800-USA-RAIL, www.amtrak. com) and MARC (1-800-325-RAIL, www. mtamaryland.com) have train service from Washington.

Two mighty rivers, the Potomac and the Shenandoah, merge at Harpers Ferry. The first European to settle at this confluence—in colonial times known as The Hole—was Peter Stephens in 1733. By 1747 the site was purchased by Robert Harper, who began a ferry service crossing the Potomac. A strategic location on the two rivers, the spot was chosen by George Washington for an arsenal: waterpower would be harnessed, firearms would be manufactured in quantity, and then easily shipped to other points. It was the arsenal that attracted John Brown and his band of abolitionists to Harpers Ferry.

On October 16, 1859, Brown led 21 compatriots (16 white men and 5 black men) on an armed raid, seizing the armory. Their long-term plan was to supply the slaves of Virginia and Maryland with arms so that they could fight their way to freedom. Within two days Brown was defeated. Fifteen of his men were killed.

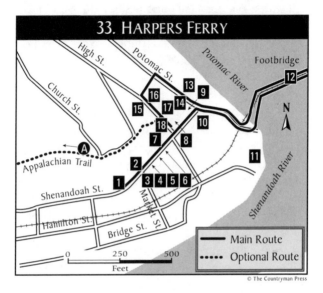

33. HARPERS FERRY

Main Route
Optional Route

Brown and the six survivors were tried and hanged in Charles Town, West Virginia.

Recognizing the town's place in American history, Congress established Harpers Ferry National Monument in 1944. Restored, much of this village is as quaint as it is historic.

This walk will concentrate on Harpers Ferry's Lower Town, much of which is within the National Historic Park. Begin at the National Park Service Visitor Center (304-535-6298, www.nps.gov/hafe). From there a shuttle bus will take you to Shenandoah Street at the foot of the historic area.

As you approach town on Shenandoah Street, use your mind's eye to transport you back to the antebellum period. The **Bookstore (1),** built in 1825, is on the left with two more retail buildings beyond. Next in the row is the **Industry Museum (2),** which is housed in a store that dates to 1845. Machines used to manufacture firearms are on display.

Opposite, at the corner of Shenandoah and Market Streets, is the **James McGraw Building (3).** Built in 1882, McGraw had a hardware store on the first floor and his living quarters above. Step inside. The exhibit "A Place in Time" relates the story of Harpers Ferry.

On leaving the museum turn right. Visit the **Provost Marshal Office (4)** next door and learn about the many law enforcement roles played by the man who used this office. Behind the **Dry Goods Store (5)** is the boardinghouse run by Mrs. Cornelia Stripes. Visit her house and view the guests' accommodations.

Your next stop should be the **Information Center (6),** which is in a redbrick house built in 1858 for the Master Armorer. Opposite the Armorer's House you'll see Frankel's Clothing Store and, next to that, the **Restoration Museum (7).** The museum provides a revealing look at the process of identifying, researching, and restoring historically significant buildings. Surprisingly, the building itself often tells much about its former occupants and uses.

Walk a few steps farther down Shenadoah Street to the corner of High Street. The building on the left has an **exhibit on Harpers Ferry wetlands (8).** Just beyond that is the **John Brown Museum (9).** A video presents the story of the man and his raid on Harpers Ferry arsenal in 1859.

After watching the video walk directly across the street to the **Arsenal or John Brown's Fort (10),** in Arsenal Square. It was originally built as a guard- and firehouse, and John Brown and his men made this their fortress toward the end of their three-day occupation. The arsenal was later moved to a farm and then to the campus of Storer College, which was founded in Harpers Ferry in 1867 primarily as a school for former slaves. John Brown's Fort was returned to the Lower Town in 1968. A plaque on its exterior reads:

> That this Nation might have a new birth of freedom,
> That slavery should be removed forever
> from American soil,
> John Brown and his 21 men gave their lives.
>
> —Alumni of Storer College, 1918

From the arsenal walk to the end of Shenandoah Street. Turn right and visit **the Point (11).** Here the two rivers converge, the Shenandoah on the right and the Potomac on the left. Note also the gap in the Blue Ridge Mountains across the way. A bridge, built in 1882, once spanned the waters on the right. The Great Flood of 1936 washed the bridge away.

The **trestle bridge (12)** on the left was completed in 1894 and supports the B & O Railroad cars as they cross the Potomac and then enter a tunnel under Maryland Heights. Parallel to the bridge is a walkway. Completed in 1985, this walkway is a part of the Appalachian Trail. Walk a bit on the bridge, turn around, and enjoy the view of town. The church on the hill is St. Peter's Roman Catholic Church, built in 1896.

From the bridge, return to town and turn right onto Potomac Street. On the right will be the **Armory's original site (13).** Opposite, on the left, will be **White Hall Tavern (14).** Built in 1838, this was a saloon frequented by the men working at the armory.

John Brown's Fort

ROBERT J. REGALBUTO

Turn left onto Hog Alley and left onto High Street. On the right will be the **Civil War Museum (15),** also a part of the national park. Opposite the museum are, descending the hill, a confectionery, an **exhibit on the 1862 Battle of Harpers Ferry (16),** A. Burton Clocks and Jewelry, and an **exhibit on Storer College (17),** "Education and the Struggle for Equality." Opposite the Storer College exhibit is another presentation: **"Black Voices" (18),** in which narrators tell stories of the struggle for freedom and equality.

Option A: The stone steps to the right lead up the hill. At the top of the steps, to the right, is the Stone House, which was built in 1782 for the town's founder, Robert Harper. The present St. Peter's Roman Catholic Church, built in 1896, replaces an earlier structure, built in 1833. From St. Peter's follow the path past St. John's Episcopal Church (1851) to Jefferson's Rock. In 1783 Thomas Jefferson stood on this spot. He took notes describing the view, which were later published in *Notes on the State of Virginia.*

Your walking tour ends here. The National Park Service has put together routes for several self-guided walks through rural areas skirting the town; itineraries and maps are available at the Information Center or on the park service web site (www.nps.gov/hafe).

V. Pennsylvania

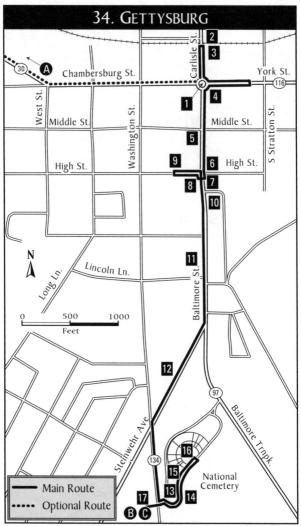

34. GETTYSBURG

Chambersburg St.

Carlisle St.

York St.

West St.

Middle St.

Washington St.

Middle St.

S Stratton St.

High St.

High St.

Baltimore St.

Long Ln.

Lincoln Ln.

N

0   500   1000
Feet

Steinwehr Ave.

Baltimore Trnpk.

National Cemetery

— Main Route
····· Optional Route

© The Countryman Press

34 · Gettysburg

Directions: *By car:* From the Capital Beltway take I-270 north to US 15 north to Gettysburg. Take Business US 15 toward downtown. Turn left onto Baltimore Street and drive to Lincoln Square. *Public transportation:* There is no public transportation to Gettysburg.

This area was settled as early as 1736 by the Getty family and others, most of whom were German or Scots-Irish. In 1786 James Getty divided his acreage into lots and founded Gettystown, which by 1800 was called Gettysburg. The town is best known for the Battle of Gettysburg, fought during the first three days of July 1863. The battle began northwest of the town, passed through it, and then continued on the southeast side. On November 18, 1863, Abraham Lincoln delivered his most famous speech. This tour begins at the site of the Gettys' homestead, passes through town, and ends at the site of the Gettysburg Address. Following the walk you could visit either Gettysburg National Military Park or the Eisenhower National Historic Site.

Start at **Lincoln Square (1).** Walk just one block north of the square on Carlisle Street and look to the right just beyond the railroad tracks. This was the **James Getty house site (2).** By coincidence, Getty, the town's founder, married Mary Todd, a cousin of Mary Todd

Lincoln. Getty's house was a log cabin that burned to the ground in 1880.

The **Gettysburg Lincoln Railroad Station (3)** is on the right. Built in 1858 in the Italianate style, the station was converted for use as a hospital during the Battle of Gettysburg. President Lincoln arrived at this station, proceeded through the town square (now Lincoln Square), and then on to the dedication ceremony at the National Cemetery, where he delivered his address. The Gettysburg Lincoln Railroad Station is currently closed for a major restoration project (717-337-3491, www.mainstreetgettysburg.org).

Return to Lincoln Square. Here and through most of this tour are waysides that provide information about historic sites.

The **David Wills House (4)** is at 6 Lincoln Square. President Lincoln stayed in this house during his visit in November 1863, and visitors may see the Lincoln Room. The house was built in 1816 and is undergoing restoration through the joint efforts of the National Park Service, the Commonwealth of Pennsylvania, the Borough of Gettysburg, and Main Street Gettysburg (717-334-8188). Some neighboring antebellum houses worth noting: the Maxwell-Danner House next door at 8 Lincoln Square and the Snell-Hoke House at number 21.

Option A: It is about a mile's excursion on Chambersburg Street to General Lee's Headquarters Museum, a stone house built in the early 19th century. Robert E. Lee chose it to be his Gettysburg base. Memorabilia and artifacts are on permanent display (717-334-3141). To reach the museum, walk to the end of Chambersburg Street and bear right on Buford Street (US 30). The museum will be on the right. En route you'll pass two schools: Shead's Oak Ridge Seminary on the right (a private girls' school built in 1862) and Gettysburg Lutheran Theological Seminary (founded in 1826) on the left.

Walk south on Baltimore Street, passing the antebellum houses at numbers 1–6. Stop at the **courthouse (5)** at the corner of Baltimore and Middle Streets. Gettysburg's first courthouse, built in 1802, stood in Lincoln Square. Demolished, this replaced it in 1859.

Walk to the corner of Baltimore and High streets. The **Adams County Public Library (6),** on the northeast corner, was used as an office by President Eisenhower while in residence at Gettysburg, especially during the days following his heart attack in 1955. The **United Presbyterian Church (7)** is across High Street. Abraham Lincoln worshiped in this church, and President Eisenhower was a member of the congregation. The **Prince of Peace Episcopal Church (8),** on the opposite side of Baltimore Street, was built as a Civil War monument, memorializing the war's casualties, both northern and southern. The interior walls of the church contain stones gathered from throughout the world.

Just steps away, at 43 West High Street, is **St. Francis Xavier Roman Catholic Church (9)** built in 1853. Its granite exterior, added in 1920, belies the historic church within. The Sisters of Charity nursed the sick and dying here, at other hospitals, and on the battlefield. Wearing large, white, starched linen headdresses resembling the wings of a flying dove, the nuns could easily be seen on battlefields obscured by fog and gunsmoke. The sisters were based in nearby Emmitsburg, Maryland, at a convent founded by St. Elizabeth Ann Seton.

National Cemetery

Return to Baltimore Street and resume your walk south. The **Eckler-Frey House (10)** will be on the left at number 242–246. Built in 1826, this is the birthplace of Jennie Wade, the only town citizen killed in the Battle of Gettysburg.

Just a few steps farther along, on the opposite side of the street, you'll see the **Schriver House (11)** at number 309. Built in 1860, the house became a Confederate outpost. Now it is a house museum, and tours are available. The Pennsylvania Historical & Museum Commission has designated the Schriver House a Historic Preservation Award Winner (717-337-2800, www. schriverhouse.com).

At the fork in the road bear right onto Steinwehr Avenue (Business US 15). Note the **Dobbin House (12)** at number 89. This stone house was built in 1776 and over the years has been used as a Presbyterian manse, a school, a station on the Underground Railroad, and a Civil War hospital.

At the next fork bear left onto Taneytown Road. Enter

the **National Cemetery (13)** on the left. Once in the cemetery, note the **bust of Abraham Lincoln (14)** on the right, modeled by Henry Bush-Brown and a part of the Lincoln Speech Memorial. The Gettysburg Address is inscribed on the memorial, which faces the **Speaker's Rostrum (15),** placed here in 1879 on the very spot where Lincoln delivered his address to a gathering of 15,000 on November 19, 1863. Take the path to the right of the rostrum. On the left you will see the towering **Soldiers National Monument (16),** which is encircled by the graves of 3,555 Union soldiers killed in the Battle of Gettysburg. An inscription on the monument reads:

> The muffled drum's sad roll has beat
> The soldier's last tattoo
> No more on life's parade shall meet
> That brave and fallen few.

Retrace your steps to the cemetery gate, and cross the street to the **National Park Service Visitor Center (17),** where this tour ends.

Option B: To visit the Eisenhower National Historic Site, purchase tickets here; transportation is provided to the house (717-338-9114, 1-877-438-8929, www.nps.gov/eise/).

Option C: Should you choose to explore the Gettysburg National Military Park, an excellent place to begin is the Cyclorama Center, which features an enormous 1883 depiction of Pickett's Charge (877-438-8929). From there you may want to take the 1-mile High Water Mark Trail, from which you could take other trails. Longer walks are the Johnny Reb Trail (3½ miles) or the Billy Yank Trail (9 miles). Or you may wish to join a bus tour from the center, or drive a self-guided auto tour. Information on all these options are available at the National Park Service Visitor Center (717-334-1124, www.nps.gov/gett).

VI. Delaware

35 · New Castle

Directions: *By car:* Take I-95 to exit 54 (DE 141 south). At the intersection of DE 9 and DE 273 turn left onto DE 9 north. Drive a half-mile to the next traffic light and bear right onto Delaware Avenue into New Castle. The courthouse is on the left. *By public transportation:* Take the DART bus #15 from Rodney Square in Wilmington (302-652-3278, 1-800-652-3278).

There were Dutch, Swedish, and Finnish plantations in the surrounding countryside when Peter Stuyvesant arrived here in 1651 and built Fort Casimir. The Dutch renamed the settlement Niew Amstel in 1655. The British took over the town in 1664, named it New Castle, and made it the regional capital. For a time this was a part of William Penn's lands. Delaware separated from Pennsylvania to become a independent state in 1776. The following year the capital was moved from New Castle to Dover.

The Great Fire of 1824 burned much of New Castle's business district. Bypassed by major railroad lines and roads later in the 19th century, New Castle declined in importance as a trade center. Fortunately, the city's seclusion saved it from development and preserved much of its 18th- and 19th-century architectural heritage. Today

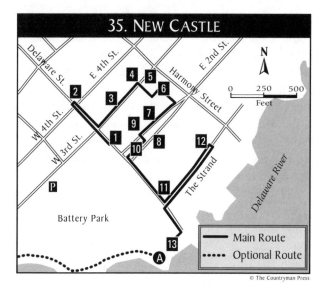

© The Countryman Press

New Castle is one of the most beautifully preserved communities on the East Coast and, many feel, a well-kept secret. Take this walking tour and see if you agree.

The **courthouse (1),** on Delaware Street between Second and Market Streets, is the starting point for this walk. Dating to 1732, it was built on the site of an earlier (1680) courthouse. The Colonial Assembly met here, and the building served as the state's capitol until 1777. The cupola marks the center of the 12-mile radius of the circular border between Delaware and Pennsylvania, and the flags that fly from the balcony (United States, Great Britain, Sweden, and the Netherlands) reflect New Castle's heritage. The New Castle Court House is open to the public for tours (302-323-4453, www.destatemuseums.org).

Resume your walk at the Henry Burgie Memorial Fountain (1895) in front of the court house. Facing Delaware Street turn right and walk to **Amstel House (2),** at the corner of Fourth Street. Built in 1738, this was the home of Governor Van Dyke. In 1784, George Washington was a guest here at the wedding reception for the governor's daughter. A well-preserved colonial mansion, Amstel House has retained many period details inside and out. Many 18th- and 19th-century New Castle antiques and artifacts are on permanent exhibit. Amstel House is one of three sites on this tour opened to the public by the New Castle Historical Society (302-322-2794, www.newcastlecity.org/nc_hs).

Retrace your steps along Delaware Street to Third Street and turn left. Stop at the **Dutch House Museum (3),** at 32 East Third Street. Another New Castle Historical Society property, this diminutive house dates to the late 17th century and is furnished with Dutch period pieces. It is open for tours by the New Castle Historical Society (302-322-2794, www.newcastlecity.org/nc_hs).

Just steps away, at 40 Third Street, is the **Old Library Museum (4),** built in 1892 as the New Castle Library. Many octagonal houses were built in the northeast at that time, but this is a rare example of an octagonal public building. Its solid redbrick exterior belies the sky-lit interior, which today houses an exhibit on New Castle's history. The Old Library Museum is also owned and maintained by the New Castle Historical Society (302-322-2794, www.newcastlecity.org/nc_hs).

Continue along Third Street to Harmony Street. The building on the left corner is the **Academy (5).** Built in 1798 as a private school, it was later used as a public

COURTESY OF NEW CASTLE COURT HOUSE MUSEUM

Courthouse

library and then a public school well into the 20th century.

Walk back to the Dutch House, cross the street, and walk along the wall that separates the green from the churchyard. The green was set aside in 1655 as a common pasture for the townspeople's livestock.

Enter the churchyard, where many of New Castle's most prominent citizens—signers of the Declaration of Independence, senators, and governors—are buried. Look at the facade of **Immanuel Church (6).** This Anglican congregation gathered in 1689, and the church was built in 1793. In the 1820s the noted American architect Richard Strickland expanded the church by adding the transepts (the arms extending from the nave) and bell tower, which houses a set of English bells. These are rung by hand just as they are in England, in a style known as change ringing. Both the bells and the church interior were restored following a fire in 1980 that left only the walls. The church's quiet, serene interior reflects Strickland's original neoclassical design (302-328-2413).

Leave the churchyard by way of the arched gate on Market Street. Turn right and walk down the cobblestone street. The **Arsenal (7)** will be on the right, built in 1809. Ammunition was stored here during the War of 1812. It was later used as a school and is now the Arsenal on the Green Restaurant (302-328-1290).

The **Presbyterian Church (8)** is across the way (302-328-3279). Its historic marker reads:

> Founded as a Dutch Reformed Church in 1657,
> this church was one of seven which organized
> the first Presbytery in America in 1706.
> The present brick meeting house was built in 1707.

As you continue your walk along the cobblestones toward Delaware Street, note the brownstone building on the right. This is the **Sheriff's House (9),** built in 1858, a remnant of a prison which stood here.

The statue of William Penn, modeled by Charles Cropper Parks, was placed here in 1984.

Walk though the archway of the **Old Town Hall (10),** built in 1823. This had been the site of New Castle's markethouses since 1655.

When you reach Delaware Street turn left, walk 1

block, and turn left onto **The Strand (11).** Once New Castle's business district, much of The Strand was destroyed by the Great Fire in 1824. Survivors of the fire include number 8. Built about 1720, it is the oldest house on the street.

The Great Fire stopped at the doorstep of the **Read House (12),** at number 42. When this Federal mansion was built for George Read II in 1801 it was the largest house in Delaware, with 22 rooms covering 14,000 square feet. In 1847 the $2^{1}/_{2}$-acre garden was created, and is now the oldest surviving garden in the state. Completely restored, the Read House is opened to the public by the Historical Society of Delaware (302-322-8411, www.hsd.org).

Retrace your steps down The Strand and turn left onto Delaware Street. Note the **Ticket Office (13)** across the way, which marks the end of this walking tour. The Ticket Office was built in 1832 for a small, local transportation system, the New Castle–Frenchtown Railroad.

Option: A 3-mile scenic walk begins at the foot of Delaware Street, running parallel to the Delaware River. You may enjoy fine water views on one side and the Battery on the other.

36 · Odessa

Directions: *By car:* From I-95 take exit 4 to
DE 1 south. Take exit 136 (Middletown/
Odessa) to DE 299. Turn left onto DE 299
east. DE 299 becomes Main Street in Odessa.
The Bruce House will be on the left at the
corner of Main and Second Streets. *By public
transportation:* Take DART bus #301 from the
11th Street side of Rodney Square in Wilmington (302-652-3278, 1-800-652-3278).
Get off at the Odessa-Middletown stop and
walk about 1 mile to the Historic Houses of
Odessa.

In the 17th century Dutch settlers named this village
Appoquinimink—a name shared with a nearby creek.
When Richard Cantwell built a toll bridge spanning
the creek in 1731, the town became Cantwell's Bridge. A
market town grew by the bridge as the site became a
thriving Delaware River port from which produce and
grain were shipped. Finally, in the early 1800s, the town
was renamed again, this time after the great Russian
port city of Odessa. And so, as local folk will tell you,
the town has had three names in three centuries. In the
mid-19th century the railroad bypassed the town, the
shipping industry declined, and Odessa became a shadow of its former self.

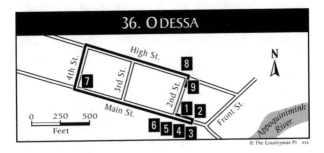

In 1938, H. Rodney Sharp bought and restored the Corbit-Sharp House (1794). This in turn led to a renewed interest in Odessa's architectural heritage and the restoration of its 18th- and 19th-century buildings, some of which you will visit on this tour.

Begin at the **Brick Hotel (1)** at the corner of Main and Second Streets. It is one of the four sites on this tour owned and operated by Winterthur Museum, Garden and Library, based in Wilmington (302-378-4069, www.winterthur.org/historic_houses). You may purchase tickets at the Javier Stable just in back of the Brick Hotel.

The hotel, built in 1822, offered accommodations and refreshments to ship captains, merchants, and others visiting the thriving port of Cantwell's Bridge in the early 19th century. It is now Winterthur's Historic Houses Visitor Center.

Next on Main Street is a house named, appropriately, **Leftovers (2).** It was constructed by H. Rodney Sharp in 1955 using the remnants and architectural details not used elsewhere in town during the restoration process.

Main Street continues on to Cantwell's Bridge, which

crosses the Appoquinimink Creek. After seeing the bridge and creek, cross Main Street and reverse your direction, back toward town. The **Frame and Log House (3),** built as a store in 1740, will be on the left. The **Pump House (4)** is next door. Both stand in the shadow of the **Corbit-Sharp House (5).** This very fine Georgian manor was built in 1772–74 for William Corbit, who made his fortune operating a tannery just steps away from this house along the banks of the creek. The house stayed in the Corbit family for more than a century and a half before being acquired by H. Rodney Sharp in 1938. Twenty years later Mr. Sharp donated the house to the Winterthur Museum. The interior has been meticulously restored and is opened to the public. The expansive grounds offer sweeping views of the Appoquinimink, and visitors may also visit the Colonial Revival gardens.

Continue along Main Street. The next house on the left is another Winterthur restoration: the **Wilson-Warner House (6).** It was built for merchant David Wilson Sr. in 1769, and its interior has been furnished using information from the house's 1829 inventory. Be sure to follow the driveway to the rear of the house and see the old skinning shack and beehive ovens.

Resume your walk down Main Street. En route you will see a variety of 18th- and 19th-century homes and businesses. Turn right onto Fourth Street. The redbrick building at the corner of Main and Fourth was built as a **public school (7)** in 1844. It is now Odessa's Community Center. Walk down Fourth Street and turn right onto High Street. The series of late-Federal-style houses on the left between Third and Fourth Streets were built in the 1840s. By contrast the late Victorian house at 209

ROBERT J. REGALBUTO

(15) The Corbit-Sharp House

High Street was built at the turn of the last century.

Stop at the corner of High and Second Streets. The **Corbit-Calloway Memorial Library (8)** is on the left. Built in 1968, this is the fourth building to house Odessa's library. Founded in 1847, it is Delaware's oldest free library.

The **Collins-Sharp House (9)** stands opposite the library. Dating to 1700, it is one of the oldest houses in Delaware. Winterthur opens the house for visitors and offers special programs, ranging from cooking classes using 18th- and 19th-century recipes to gardening and other outdoor activities.

You have come full circle and completed this walking tour; the Javier stable and the Brick Hotel are just a few steps away.

37 · Dover

Directions: *By car:* From I-95 take exit 4 (DE 1 south). Take exit 104 to US 13 south for 3 miles to Court Street. Turn right onto Court Street; Legislative Hall will be on the left. *By public transportation:* Take DART bus #301 from the 11th Street side of Rodney Square in Wilmington (302-652-3278, 1-800-652-3278).

William Penn gave the order to establish Dover as a county seat in 1683 and named it after the English port city. The streets were laid in 1717. A marketing center for the surrounding farms grew around the courthouse. Delaware's capital was moved here from New Castle in 1777 and a decade later, on December 7, 1787, Delaware became the first state to ratify the Constitution.

Begin your walking tour at **Legislative Hall (1).** Constructed in 1933 and incorporating Georgian Revival details, the hall was twice expanded (1970 and 1994) and completely renovated in 1997. Delaware's senate and house of representatives meet here. The hall also houses the governor's ceremonial office and a large collection of portraits. Tours are given, but it is advisable to call in advance for schedule information (302-739-4114, 1-800-282-8565, www.state.de.us/research/assembly.htm).

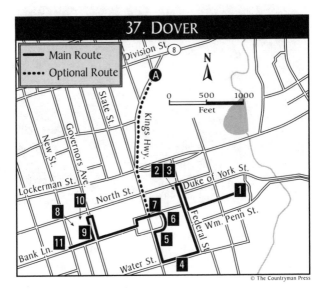

© The Countryman Press

Leave the hall at Legislative Avenue and walk the length of Legislative Mall, which is the scene of many festivals and special events. At the end of the mall walk to the corner on the right, Federal and North Streets. The **Delaware State Visitor Center (2)** has two galleries displaying changing exhibits by local artists and collections of artifacts, costumes, and arts and crafts. The center also houses a gift shop (302-739-4266, www.destatemuseums.org).

The center is contiguous with the **Biggs Museum of American Art (3).** The museum's 14 galleries feature the private collection of its founder, Sewell C. Biggs. Two centuries of paintings, spanning the colonial era through Impressionism, are on display, including works by American artists Gilbert Stuart, Thomas Cole, Childe

Quill and Cube, Constitution Park

Hassam, Albert Bierstadt, and the Peales. The decorative arts collection, which includes furniture and silver, focuses on works created by Delaware craftsmen. American drawings, sculpture, ceramics, and needlework complete the collection (302-674-2111, www.biggsmuseum.org).

Return to Federal Street, turn right, and walk to Water Street. **Christ Church (4)** will be in front of you on the right. In 1703 a group of 22 local citizens sent a petition to the Church of England's Society for the Propagation of the Gospel in Foreign Parts, requesting the ministry of an Anglican priest. After his arrival the parish's first church was built in 1707—10 years before there were streets. The present church was built in 1734 and over the years has been enlarged and remodeled. Caesar Rodney, a member of Christ Church and a signer of the Declaration of Independence, is memorialized in the graveyard (302-734-5731).

From Water Street turn right onto State Street and

walk to the Green. The **Kent County Court House (5)** will be on the right. Built in 1874, it stands on the site of two colonial structures: the King George Tavern and the original courthouse, built in 1694.

The **Old State House (6)** stands at the head of the Green. Dating to 1792, the Old State House was restored in 1976. The interior features a grand staircase, the Governor's Room, legislative chambers, and a courtroom. Tours of the Old State House begin at the Delaware State Visitor Center (302-739-4266, www.de-statemuseums.org).

With your back to the Old State House, face the Green. **Constitution Park (7)** is on the right. Its artwork, *Quill and Cube* (1988), is the work of Rick Rothrock and commemorates Delaware's ratification of the Constitution on December 7, 1787. A sign at the corner of the Green and State Street marks the site of the Golden Fleece Tavern where the signing took place.

Option: Woodburn, the official residence of Delaware's governor, is open by appointment (302-739-5656). To reach Woodburn turn right onto State Street, cross Lockerman Street and the Plaza, and then turn right on Kings Highway. Woodburn is at number 51. Built in 1790, the mansion later became a stop on the Underground Railroad. The mansion's formal garden, planted with boxwood, trees, and flowers, is open to the public.

Return to the Green and walk to the far end, continuing down Bank Lane. Cross Governors Avenue to **Meeting House Square (8),** which was commissioned by William Penn and planned by his surveyors in 1717. On the left is the former Presbyterian Church. Built in 1790, it replaced an earlier log meetinghouse which stood on the site. Now a museum, **Meeting House Gallery I (9)** has a permanent exhibit that focuses on 12,000 years of archaeology in Delaware. The church's former Sunday school, built next door in 1880, is now the **Meeting House Gallery II (10).** Its Main Street Delaware exhibit illustrates small town life a century ago and includes a general store and printing presses. A third museum in the Square is the **Johnson Victrola Museum (11).** E. R. Johnson, a Delaware native, founded the Victrola Talking Machine Company. The museum features victrolas, musicians, and their recordings from the first quarter of the 20th century. All three museums share this site with the historic Presbyterian cemetery (302-739-4266, www.destatemuseums.org).

Your Dover walking tour ends here, leaving you free to explore and enjoy the museums. Return to Legislative Hall by way of Bank Lane, the Green, and Legislative Mall.

Also Nearby

Delaware Agricultural Museum and Village (302-734-1618)

Delaware State Police Museum and Educational Center (302-739-7700)

Air Mobility Command Museum (302-677-5938)

John Dickinson Plantation (302-739-3277)

38 · Lewes

Directions: *By car:* From I-95 take exit 4.
Drive on DE 1 south to US 9 east (Savannah
Road) into downtown Lewes. Turn right onto
East Third Street and then right onto King's
Highway. The Fisher Martin House will be on
the right. *By public transportation:* Other than
the ferry from Cape May, New Jersey, there is
no public transportation to Lewes.

Lewes, first settled by the Dutch in 1631, justifiably
boasts that it was the first town in the first state.
Originally named Zwaanendael (the Valley of the
Swans) after a Dutch town, it was renamed Lewes in
1685, taking its name from a town in Sussex, England.
A seaport for more than three centuries, Lewes has been
a whaling center, a port of call for Captain Kidd and
other pirates, and a target for the British during the War
of 1812. Today it is home to a fleet of fishing boats, bay
and river pilots, and a ferry terminus opposite Cape
May, New Jersey.

This tour begins at the **Fisher Martin House (1),**
at 120 King's Highway. Dating to 1730, the house was
built for the Quaker Thomas Fisher on land granted by
William Penn. It was acquired by Scots-Irish Presbyterian minister James Martin in 1736. The Fisher-Martin
House is open to the public and serves as Lewes Visitor

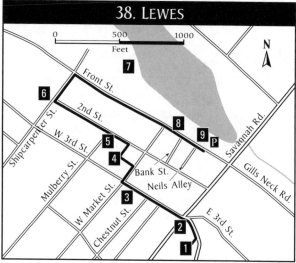

38. LEWES

© The Countryman Press

and Information Center (302-645-8073, 1-877-465-3937, www.leweschamber.com). Be sure to visit the herb garden alongside the house. As you leave the property, look across King's Highway to the Lewes Presbyterian Church, founded in 1692; the present church dates to 1832. The churchyard has the graves of many notable Delaware citizens, including governors.

From the door of the Fisher-Martin House turn left. At the corner you will see the **Zwaanendael Museum (2).** The museum was built in 1931 to commemorate the 300th anniversary of the arrival of the Dutch. The inspiration for the building was the *stadhuis* (city hall) in Hoorn, Holland. Step inside to see permanent and changing exhibits that highlight the area's history, artifacts, and culture, including the original Dutch settlement, the British bombardment during the War of 1812, shipwrecks, and the Cape Henlopen Lighthouse (302-645-1148).

From the front door of the museum turn left and walk down Third Street to number 116, the **Old Fire House and Jail (3)** built in 1897. The jail housed prisoners of war during World War II. Next door, at number 114, is a private enterprise know as the Preservation Forge. Wrought iron products are crafted and sold from this operating blacksmith shop (302-645-7987).

Continue along West Third Street to West Market Street. Turn right, and **St. Peter's Church (4)** will be on the left, an Episcopal Church built in 1858. Its congregation first gathered in 1681. Walk through the graveyard. Four Delaware governors are buried here. The oldest stone in the churchyard reads:

> Here lyeth ye body
> of Margaret ye widow
> of James Huling who
> desest Febry ye 16th
> in ye 76 yeare of her age. 1707
> Born 1631

Leave the front entrance of St. Peter's churchyard, turn left on Second Street, and walk to the **Ryves Holt House (5),** at number 218. Built in 1665, this is the oldest house in Delaware and the Visitor Information Center for the Lewes Historical Society. This walking tour includes a visit to their complex and museum, and tickets may be purchased here (302-645-7670, www.historiclewes.org/).

Turn left from the Ryves Holt House and walk to the end of Second Street. Cross Shipcarpenter Street to the

Lewes Historical Society Complex (6). The complex includes the following:

- Thompson Country Store was built in Thompsonville, Delaware, in 1800 and moved to this site in 1963. The Ellegood House (a gift shop) and a blacksmith shop are in back of the store.
- Burton-Ingram House—built about 1769, the house has fine period woodwork within and without, and houses a museum of portraits, furniture, and artifacts that illustrate the city's early history.
- The Rabbit's Ferry House dates to the mid-18th century. A farmhouse built in the rural area of Rabbit's Ferry in Sussex County, it was moved here in 1967.
- The Early Plank House is a Swedish log house built in the 1600s.
- The Doctor's Office (circa 1850) stands behind the Early Plank House. Used as a physician's office for many years, it is now a museum of 19th-century medicine and dentistry.
- The Midway School is a late-19th-century one-room schoolhouse. It originally stood on a country road between Lewes and Rehoboth.
- The Hiram Rodney Burton House was built about 1780 and is filled with period furnishings. The house also contains the Lewes Historical Society's library and archives.

Exit the complex on Shipcarpenter Street. As you look to the right you will see Shipcarpenter Square, a community of restored 18th- and 19th-century houses moved to this site. Turn left and walk to the end of Shipcarpenter Street to the **lightship** *Overfalls* **(7),** which is docked on the Lewes Rehoboth Canal. Commis-

Zwaanendael Museum

sioned in 1938, this was the last lightship built by the United States Lighthouse Service. Decommissioned in 1972, the *Overfalls* is on the National Register of Historic Places and is open to visitors by the *Overfalls* Maritime Museum Foundation (302-644-8050, www.overfalls. org). The U.S. Lifesaving Station nearby was built in 1884.

Walk along Front Street parallel to the canal. The **Cannonball House Marine Museum (8)** will be on the right at number 118. Built before 1787, this house is named for the British cannonball that hit it during the

War of 1812. The museum is maintained by the Lewes Historical Society, and its garden is the handiwork of the Sussex Gardeners (302-645-7670).

The **1812 Memorial Park (9)** is on the opposite side of Front Street. Lewes was bombarded by the British on April 6 and 7, 1813. The park has several guns that were fired in defense of the town.

Your tour ends here. You may wish to turn left onto Savannah Road, cross the canal, and visit Lewes public beach on Delaware Bay. Alternately, a right on Savannah Road will bring you to the many shops and restaurants along Second Street.

Index